THE ATLANTIC COAST OF
IRELAND

THE ATLANTIC COAST OF
IRELAND

Photography by Jonathan Hession
Text by John Grenham

F

FRANCES LINCOLN LIMITED

PUBLISHERS

Frances Lincoln Limited
74–77 White Lion Street
London N1 9PF
www.franceslincoln.com

The Atlantic Coast of Ireland
Copyright © Frances Lincoln Limited 2014
Photographs copyright © Jonathan Hession 2014
Text copyright © John Grenham 2014
Design by Ger Garland

First Frances Lincoln edition 2014

A catalogue record for this book is available from the
British Library.

ISBN 9780711235793

Printed and bound in China

1 2 3 4 5 6 7 8 9

HALF TITLE PAGE:
Dunmore Head evening view of the Great Blasket
Island, Kerry

FULL TITLE PAGE:
View of Connemara from Inishmore, Galway.

Contents

This book is for Jane Powers.

ACKNOWLEDGEMENTS

My gratitude goes to Jo Christian who commissioned this book and
my best friend John who did the brainy bit and wrote the words.
I would also like to express my thanks to my very good friend
Brendan Gunn for his great company and hospitality in Donegal.
My thanks to Pascal Bradley for his chatter on the hills and Margaret
Duffy for looking after me so very well at their house in Galway.
And my gratitude goes to Pat Hickey for allowing me to use his
portrait, Neil Ryan in The Office of Public Works for his enthusiastic
assistance and Frank Miller for his time and helpful suggestions.
And finally, to Ger Garland for the lovely book design.

JONATHAN HESSION, 2014

INTRODUCTION

Look at a large-scale map of the Atlantic and it's clear that a very long time ago this ocean did not exist. The north-east shoulder of Brazil tucks neatly into the African Gulf of Guinea. The western bulge of Africa matches the great sunken bay of the Caribbean. Europe, south-west to north-east, lines up almost precisely against the coast of North America, south-east to north-west. However long ago it might have been, these two great land-masses were clearly attached to each other. Their slow peeling apart is what has allowed the ocean to come into being.

Look at a smaller scale map of Britain and Ireland. Again, it's obvious that the two islands were once joined, with the coastlines of western Britain and eastern Ireland echoing an ancient separation across the Irish Sea.

Then look at the Atlantic coast of Ireland. You may search the map as long as you like, but you won't find anything, anywhere, that fits with it. And that simple fact of geography tells you a lot about this extraordinary place. It has been in the front line of the elemental battle between sea and land for so long that its very shape is an accumulation of scar-tissue. The peninsulas amputated and eroded by tide and wind, the granite mountains gnawed at steadily until they turn into sea-cliffs, the crazy scattering of inlets and islands twisted into and around each other, all speak of immense, slow-motion violence inflicted on this land.

All landscapes reflect and embody the natural and human powers that created them. If you want to experience the historical depth of the natural processes of geology and weather, to feel the sheer scale of the unending change they generate, this shoreline is one of the best places on the planet to do it. The effects of deep time echo here as vividly as possible, in storm-clouds and waves, in mountain-peaks and limestone caves.

However much it draws our imagination towards vast, inhuman forces and timescales, this landscape is also overlain with an inescapable layer of human history. Ecology, invasions, climate change, agriculture, religion, popular culture – all of these shaped the particularity and identity of place and peoples along the coast. History is embedded everywhere here, on every scale. Tens of millions of stories, some tiny, some epic, went to make each limestone flag, the shape of each peak, the camber of each sodden field. The aftertaste of those stories still hangs in the Atlantic air.

Jonathan Hession's photographs of this coast are perfectly-framed, self-contained instants, superbly deep and pellucid. They feel utterly timeless. But in fact they are flawless slivers of the most time-filled of narratives, ranging through the vastness of geology to the small-scale dramas of superstition and local conflict. In all of the pictures, though humanity is offstage, there is an aching attraction to the place itself. They evoke a strong desire to get out into those huge Atlantic spaces, to be inside their sheer difference. To restore the sense of life that only such enormous, unending transience can provide.

DONEGAL
Dún na nGall

DONEGAL

Donegal clings to the Republic by a thread. Only a thin sliver of coast, dominated by the lurid, knees-up neon of Bundoran, connects the county with the South. Otherwise it is pure Ulster, oriented culturally, socially and economically to the east, towards Northern Ireland. The people speak with the syncopation and the slow, stretched, inverted vowels of Ulster. But the Donegal accent is strangely mild: the further north you go, the more elongated the lilt, the softer and more exaggerated the verbal gestures become. In a petrol station in Letterkenny or a pub in Dunfanaghy, it can be hard not to hear this as pure, limp-wristed camp. It's not. These people speak very gently, but they're tough.

Misunderstanding runs in the opposite direction, too. Some of the most violent place-names in Ireland are here: Bloody Foreland, jutting out into the naked North Atlantic, surely named for the ferocity of its battering by the sea; the Poisoned Glen, bleak, empty, lifeless. In fact, the Foreland (*Cnoc na Fola*) is so called because of the extraordinary rusty red that it radiates in the evening sunlight. And The Poisoned Glen is a wonderful example of mistranslation. *Cró Nimhe* or *Cró Nemhe*? The latter means Heavenly Glen, and that's what the locals insist is its real name.

There is no denying the often startling violence of Donegal's Atlantic coast, however. Along the northern edge, with no shelter from the ocean, millennia of attack by storms have gnawed sharp fissures into the land: Sheephaven Bay, Broadwater Lough, Mulroy Bay, and the magnificent Lough Swilly, stretching 40 km inland. Travelling distances are very deceptive here – rounding those deep inlets can turn five minutes as-the-crow-flies into a two-hour meander.

Heading south and west, the land fights back, producing some of the most spectacular scenery in all of Ireland, the sheer precarious obstinacy of the cliffs at Horn Head contrasting with the vast deserted crescents of the beaches at Downies.

Further south again, and the to-and-fro between sea and rock continues. Shelter at Gweedore and Ardara and Dungloe is carved out by the sea. The cliffs of Slieve League on the Glencolumbkille promonotory resist. And over them all, louring in the background are the great bleak mountains of Muckish, Errigal and Slieve Snacht (the Snow Mountain).

PREVIOUS PAGES:
Slieve League cliffs in S.W. Donegal. Rising to 601m these sea cliffs are the second highest in Ireland. The 'One Man's Path' a very narrow ridge on the route to the summit of Slieve League can be a place of vertiginous horror on account of the severe drops on either side.

The Poisioned Glen.
Originally called the in Irish 'The Heavenly
Glen' this beautiful valley is the access route
for walkers intending to climb Slieve Snaght.

Malin Head

Malin Head is the most northerly point of the island of Ireland. It is thus further north than the North, Northern Ireland, although it remains part of the South, the Republic, and is self-evidently therefore the most northerly part of the South. Welcome to Ireland, where borders zig-zag through names and language, disappear, resurface, dissolve.

Just 50 km north of Malin across the Sea of Moyle lies the Scottish island of Islay. For those dozens of centuries when sea-travel was the only realistic mode of transport, this was not a boundary but a connection – goods, soldiers, monks, language and culture flowed freely back and forth and those deep connections still exist. The Irish language ('Gaelic' in Scotland), the strong clan and tribal connections, the way of life centred on fishing and subsistence farming, the music, the storytelling, even the enthusiasm for illicit distilling – these are all shared across what has become an international border. The people of north-west Donegal and Islay can look at each other as distorting mirrors that show the outlines of alternative history. One fewer defeat and we could be you.

But the Sea of Moyle is not easy water. When a North Atlantic winter depression deepens explosively and a January storm collapses in from the north-east, lashed on by bitter winds that have met no other obstacle for 5,000 km, the sea is the stuff of nightmares. Here it was that the children of Lír, transformed into swans by their vindictive stepmother, had to spend 300 years awaiting release from the spell. Even compared to the rest of the Atlantic coast, where winter storms can be breathtaking, winter on the Sea of Moyle was a byword for misery.

Many listeners to BBC radio are familiar with Malin as part of the great litany of exotic headlands and seas – 'Bailey, Rockall, Malin, Hebrides . . .' – that makes up the Shipping Forecast broadcast four times a day. And this familiarity has changed the name. In the mouths of the locals, it is *Máilin*, the little headland, pronounced 'Mawlin', but for the sake of peace, for not having to explain for the umpteenth time, now they too use the BBC version, at least when speaking to outsiders.

LEFT:
Farm at Malin Head. Living on Ireland's most northern stony headland allows for little beyond the basic necessities.

OPPOSITE ABOVE:
Horn Head Cliffs. Just north of Dunfanaghy, the 3 hour walk around Horn Head has fantastic views, blowholes, wildlife and flora. This is designated as a 'Special Area of Conservation' by the Irish government.

Doe Castle

Doe Castle was built by the Mac Suibhne na dTuaith, the MacSweeney Doe, in the early sixteenth century. Their story illustrates just how complex the migrations back and forth between the two islands could be. Their forebears arrived in Ireland from Scotland in the thirteenth century to work as 'gallowglasses', mercenary soldiers, for the native Irish O'Donnell dynasty. They may have been forced out by a Norse invasion of Scotland or as part of a dispute with the Scottish king, Alexander III. In any case, they were reluctant migrants. But they spoke Gaelic and the culture they became part of in Donegal was a mirror image of their own: a dominant part of their Scottish inheritance came from the fifth-century invasion of Western Scotland by the Irish.

They had other ancestors, however, most conspicuously the Vikings who had raided and settled down the Western Isles for almost three centuries. The mixture of warlike Celtic tribesmen and Nordic warriors produced a strain of people for whom fighting and hospitality were second nature. The MacSweeneys typified the breed. Before long, they had taken payment from the O'Donnells in the form of vast areas of the O'Donnells' own land in the north-west and established their own franchise, splitting into three Gaelic chieftainships, moving across Donegal from south-east to north-west: MacSweeney Banagh, MacSweeney Fanad and MacSweeney Doe.

With the final collapse of the Gaelic aristocracy in the seventeenth century, all three lines died out. The last of the MacSweeney Does, Maol Muire (Myles), joined the English attack on Red Hugh O'Donnell in 1598, and over the course of just three years was defeated and then knighted by Elizabeth I; joined O'Donnell but was captured by the English; escaped and rejoined O'Donnell; surrendered to the English, then took up arms against them again. In 1604 he was pardoned. In 1608 he was charged with treason. Somehow he managed to get a grant of 2,000 acres in the plantation of Ulster. Miraculously, in 1630 he still had possession of these lands, but the wars of the rest of the century destroyed the family's wealth.

The original import of gallowglasses was necessary to fight the Normans, invited to Ireland by the King of Leinster, Dermot Mac Murrough, to fight on his behalf. And, of course, the Normans were also descended from the Vikings: the mercenaries on both sides had overlapping ancestry. And, of course, the result was the same as everywhere else where foreign warriors were used as the military servants of a ruling class. As in Rome and Renaissance Italy, as with the Mamluks in Turkey, as with the Chinese in the Middle Ages, soldiers hired to fight for you will eventually rule you.

OPPOSITE ABOVE:
Looking north across McSwyne's Bay, an inlet in southern Donegal with wonderful views of the Slieve League cliffs to the north and Saint John's Point to the south.

OPPOSITE BELOW:
Doe Castle at Sheephaven Bay.

Geology of the North-West

Geologically, Ireland is divided very distinctly in two. 450 million years ago north-west Ireland was part of a the landmass of Laurentia, which is now mainly represented in North America. The rest of the island, south and east of a line drawn from Galway to Belfast, lay beyond an ocean several thousand miles to the south: it belonged to a different tectonic plate. As the two plates moved together, one being squeezed under the other at enormous pressure, a mountain-building phase developed, analogous to the plate-collision that continues to raise the Alps and the Himalayas. In geology, the process has become known as the Caledonian (after the Latin name for Scotland) orogeny (mountain-creation). And the mountains of Donegal, west Mayo and west Galway are indeed the siblings of the Highlands of Scotland, but also of the range that runs the length of the Scandinavian peninsula as well as of the mountains of eastern Greenland. All share the same north-east to south-west orientation, embodying the direction of the single force that created them all. The only thing that has separated the family is time, as it does all families.

The scales of time required for Ireland, Scotland, Greenland and Scandinavia to drift thousands of kilometres apart are almost literally unimaginable, a problem faced by everyone trying to understand geology. The Caledonian orogeny is not the only, or perhaps even the main, cause of what we see when we look at Errigal or Slieve League or Croagh Patrick. Before the mountains were slowly crushed upwards half a billion years ago, the material they are made of, their stone, already existed. In a few parts of Donegal, West Mayo and West Galway, this rock was igneous granite, formed by the upwelling of molten magma, extraordinarily dense and resistant to erosion. The rocks at Bloody Foreland and underlying Gola Island, Gweedore and parts of far north-west Donegal are the contorted results of mountain-making on this granite.

But most of the pre-existing rock was sedimentary, laid down in warm shallow seas over the course of hundreds of millions of the preceding years. For most of Donegal, this sediment was sand, falling particle on to particle, for thousands of centuries, until the very weight of the sand itself forced out all air and water between individual particles and solidified them. This was sandstone.

The immense heat and pressure created by the slow, titanic crushing together of the continental plates in the Caledonian orogeny changed the sandstone. The most common component of sand, the crystalline mineral silica, better known as quartz, was compressed to the point where its individual crystals fused. It became quartzite, intensely hard, intensely resistant. Errigal, stubborn and unchanging, is quartzite. So are Croagh Patrick and Nephin in Mayo, and the Twelve Bens in Connemara.

And after the mountains were made, change continued – geographic change as the chain was slowly ripped asunder by the continents, climate change as glaciation came and went. Each glacial episode compressed the rock as the ice sitting on it grew to depths of tens of kilometres, so heavy that the ice began to de-form and to flow. As it flowed over the earth's cracked surface, the ice softened and lifted lumps of rock, incorporating them into the ice itself. In this way, sediments of all sizes became part of the glacier's load. Then these rocks themselves, frozen into the bottom of the ice, acted like the grit in sandpaper, abrading and polishing everything they passed over. Even after the glacial ice retreated, change continued. Hundreds of centuries of rain, wind and ice chafed the rocks, bringing up the hard, wiping away the soft.

Every peak and valley from Malin to Galway, every inlet, every lake and hillock is the utterly unique outcome of the accumulation of billions of changes. Some were huge, some were infinitesimal. They continue on time-scales we can only glimpse from the corner of our eyes, outside the range of human perception. And they are still happening.

Surnames

One feature of Ireland as a whole, and not just the coast, is the deep connection between particular surnames and particular areas. This is not the kind of connection embodied in toponymic names such as Crawford ('the ford of the crow') or Da Vinci ('from Vinci'). Irish surnames are not descriptive of a geographic origin; rather, they are linked to former tribal areas. As ever in Ireland, who you're related to is much more important than where precisely you're from.

One result is great concentrations of the same name in a particular area, as conspicuous and characteristic over the local pubs and shops as the mountains and the sea. And the surnames encode the changes undergone by the people who bear them.

Donegal, for example, is *Tír Chonaill* in Irish, literally 'Conall's land'. This Conall was one of the sons of the fifth-century King Niall Noigeallach ('Nine-hostage-holding Niall'). From Niall came the great tribal grouping that dominated the north and east of the island for more than four centuries in the early middle ages, the *Uí Néill*, 'descendants of Niall'. Inevitably, this great tribe splintered and one split was between the followers of two of his sons: the *Cenel Chonaill* ('people of Conall') and the *Cenel Eoghain* ('people of Eoghan'). Hence *Tír Chonaill* and, at the root of the modern county name of Tyrone, *Tír Eoghainn*.

All of this was long before hereditary surnames existed, but when the Gaelic aristocracy began to adopt surnames in the eleventh century, the old tribal allegiances were still very much alive, and certain surnames were marked in the public mind as belonging to specific groups. This understanding persisted through oral tradition, helped by the Gaelic fascination with the construction of genealogies, and survives today.

In Donegal, the Gallaghers, the Dohertys, the O'Donnells, the Boyles, the Breslins and the Gilbrides all know themselves as part of the *Cenel Chonaill*. In most cases, they also know at what point their particular branch budded off from the main stem. All Gaelic Irish surnames are patronymic, deriving from a father or grandfather. Gallagher is *Ó Gallcobhair*, 'grandson of Gallcobhar', from *gall*, meaning 'foreign' and *cabhar* meaning 'help' – a Scottish mercenary, perhaps; O'Donnell is *Ó Domhnaill*, grandson of Donal, a forename meaning 'world-mighty'; Gilbride is *Mac Giolla Bhríde*, 'son of the follower of (St) Bridget'. Each surname points to a single originator, and in most cases family tradition and medieval genealogy names that individual. So the Dohertys, for example, claim descent from one Dochartach who lived in the tenth century and has traditionally been claimed as twelfth in lineal descent from Conall.

In what sense is this accurate? The status of folk-knowledge in Ireland is pretty well summarised in the response of the old Irishwoman asked by W. B. Yeats if she believed in fairies: 'Of course I don't believe in them. But they exist.' So is there any way of investigating these traditions scientifically?

Surprisingly, there is. In 2005, the professor of genetics at Trinity College Dublin, Dan Bradley (a common anglicisation of the fine *Cenel Eoghain* surname Ó Brolcháin), took 53 men with surnames that traditionally belong to the *Uí Néill* grouping and examined their DNA. He took advantage of a happy coincidence between culture and science: the Y-chromosome is passed from father to son in a way that mimics precisely the patri-lineal inheritance of surnames. Small mutations occur in the Y-chromosome from time to time (SNPs, single nucleotide polymorphisms, if you want to impress your friends) and each of these mutations is then passed on with the Y-chromosome to the son and the son's sons and so on forever. Because they persist and accumulate, examining when Y-chromosome SNPs came into existence can reveal the period when the most recent common ancestor of any group of men lived. And it turned out that there was strong

The dunes at Tramore Strand gradually morph into agricultural land.

evidence for a common ancestor for a significant proportion of this particular group seventeen centuries ago, the period when Niall Noigeallach lived. Extrapolating from it, the TCD group estimated that as many as 21 per cent of the male population of north-west Ireland were descended from this common ancestor.

One perk of Gaelic chieftainship was the right to indulge your fertility, and the popular interpretation of the DNA study was that Niall was a bit of a lad. But of course the study tells us nothing so specific, or interesting. The common ancestor could just as easily have been a lowly pot-bearer whose grandchildren all got royal flushes in the game of genetic poker. In any case, seventeen centuries represents between fifty and sixty generations and each generation means a doubling of the number of ancestors and a dilution of the genome. What the likely lads in the north-western 21 per cent inherited from Niall can be no more that one ten-thousandth of their genetic make-up.

Suggestive (and unproveable) as such a study is, further investigations of great concentrations of Irish surnames have come to the widest possible range of conclusions. Ryan (from Ó Maoilriagháin, 'grandson of [a devotee of St] Riaghan') originated separately from multiple men at different times. O'Sullivan (Ó Suileabháin, deriving from *súil*, eye, and taken to mean either 'one-eyed' or 'hawk-eyed', depending on whether you are an O'Sullivan) appears to have an origin similar to the *Uí Néill* in a single individual, but much later. McMahon (from Mac Mathghamha, from *mathghamhain*, meaning 'bear') stems from two distinct individuals, one in Clare, the other in Monaghan.

But the most interesting surnames are not the most numerous. Intensely localised names still continue in very specific places. Every Lavelle and every Kilbane almost certainly comes from, or has connections to, Achill Island. You will find Mungovans nowhere but west Clare. If you tell an Irish person your name is Sugrue or Fitzmaurice, they'll presume you're from Kerry. And you can't throw a stone in west Cork without hitting a Harrington.

'Bradley' illustrates just how a name can embody the history undergone by those who bear it. In form it is purely English, derived from the village of Bradley in Lincolnshire. But in Ireland it was originally Ó Brolcháin. It's hard not to imagine an overworked and monolingual English record-keeper just giving up and saying, 'No, your name is not whatever you said, it's Bradley. You're all Bradleys.'

OPPOSITE ABOVE:
Waders feed on Tramore Strand under the shadow of Muckish Mountain.

OPPOSITE BELOW:
Dunes on Maghera Strand.

The summit of Errigal (751m). This
mountain dominates the landscape of
north west Donegal.

<small>OPPOSITE:</small>
The plateau at the top of Muckish
Mountain.

Shrines at Mamore Gap.

Sunset over Slieve Snaght.

Ballymastocker Beach runs for over two
miles between Knockalla Hill to Port Salon
on the Fanad Peninsula. Donegal currently
boasts 13 Blue Flag beaches, the highest of
all counties in Ireland.

Ards Forest Park. Lying between
Creeslough and Dunfanaghy, Ards Forest
Park offers 480 hectares to explore.

OPPOSITE ABOVE:
An often-flooded field between Rathmullen
and Ramelton on the banks of Lough Swilly.

OPPOSITE BELOW:
Lough Swilly on a winter's day at low tide.

FOLLOWING PAGES:
Lough Altan as seen from Errigal.

Bundoran. This is the most southerly coastal town in County Donegal, an oasis of amusement centres, bouncy castles and surf schools in a desert of natural beauty.

OPPOSITE ABOVE:
St. John's Point lighthouse was established in 1833 and casts a light on the end of one of Ireland's longest peninsulas.

OPPOSITE BELOW:
Fanad Head lighthouse has been guiding mariners on the North Atlantic into Lough Swilly since 1817. It was constructed after HMS Saldanha, a frigate based in Lough Swilly, foundered on the rocks at Fanad Head in 1811. All 253 lives on board, with the exception of the ship's parrot, were lost.

PREVIOUS PAGES:
The view of the north coast of Donegal from the summit of Muckish with Dunfanaghy and Downies in the distance.

Ramelton Quay. Ramelton was one of Donegal's most prosperous towns. With access through Lough Swilly to the open sea, Ramelton became a center of international trade, much boosted by having Ulster's largest linen bleaching works during the heyday of the linen industry in the north of Ireland.

Opposite above and below:
Fort Dunree was originally built at the northern end of Lough Swilly in 1798 to defend against seaborne invasion by the French. During WW1 the fort protected Admiral Lord Jellicoe's fleet which anchored in Lough Swilly prior to the Battle of Jutland.

The fort was officially handed over to Ireland in 1936.

Saint John's Point. A skinny finger-like peninsula reaches over 10k out into Donegal Bay from the town of Dunkineely with a single road leading to Saint John's Point. This place is particularly attractive to sub-aqua divers on account of its clear waters, and with tourists in search of wonderful views both north and south.

OPPOSITE ABOVE :
Sunset south of Donegal town.

OPPOSITE BELOW:
Evening on Tramore Strand.

SLIGO
Sligeach

SLIGO

The Irish writer Benedict Kiely, who had walked and written about almost every corner of Ireland, was once asked to choose the loveliest county on the island. The implied options were the usual suspects: Cork, Kerry, Clare, Galway and Donegal. 'Sligo,' he replied, and went on to explain that it was unique in having some of everything that was beautiful in the country: mountains, lakes, beaches, rivers, woods . . . Small, overlooked Sligo has them all.

The county was created in 1579 in the Tudor re-conquest and took its name from the principal town, which was in turn named after the river running through it: the onomatopoeic *sligeach*, meaning 'full of shells'. That is the river now known as the Garavogue.

The town is situated in the right angle between the two halves of the county. To the north, the southern shores of Donegal Bay take the full brunt of the Atlantic, with the weirdly straight lines of Ben Bulben sitting majestically high in the background. This is the area traditionally held to be the home of the Fianna, the band of aristocratic warriors led by Finn McCool whose exploits form the basis of *an Fhiannaíocht*, the Fenian Cycle, one of the two great bodies of stories in pre-Christian Gaelic mythology. Not coincidentally, this district is also inextricably linked with the name of W. B. Yeats, the Nobel prize-winning poet, who spent much of his boyhood in Sligo town and used this landscape and culture in his most famous work. He is buried in Drumcliff churchyard, his gravestone bearing the epitaph he composed himself as the final words of his last published poem, 'Under Ben Bulben':

> 'Cast a cold eye
> On life, on death.
> Horseman, pass by!'

The southern half of the coast switches orientation completely, going east–west, running in almost a straight line from Ballysadare Bay to Inishcrone, and thus finessing the worst of the Atlantic storms. The landscape here has figured in sacred ritual for at least 5,000 years, with dozens of Neolithic tombs forming part of great patterns based on the seasonal movements of the sun, moon and stars, patterns whose meaning we can only guess at.

In historic times, the territory was under the control of the MacDermots, whose power was usurped by the Norman de Burgos from the twelfth to the fourteenth centuries. It was then claimed by a branch of the O'Connors, who ruled under the patronage of the northern O'Donnells, and became known as the O'Connor Sligo.

OPPOSITE ABOVE:
The view of Knocknarea and Ballysadare Bay from the sand-dunes of Strandhill.

OPPOSITE BELOW:
Drumcliff Church. The remains of Nobel Prize winner for Literature W.B. Yeats 1865-1939 are buried in this churchyard, overlooked by Ben Bulben.

PREVIOUS PAGES:
Ben Bulben's decaying north face. Part of the Dartry range of mountains, Ben Bulben was formed about 320 million years ago. It is composed mainly of lime-stone.

The Famine

The potato was the first true miracle food. A few kilos a day, along with a litre of buttermilk, and you have every nutrient the human body needs. Because of this, the accounts of travellers in the West of Ireland in the eighteenth and early nineteenth centuries are full of puzzled juxtapositions: on the one hand the vast majority of the population were destitute to a degree unheard of in the rest of western Europe, dressed in filthy rags and living in unspeakable hovels; on the other, they were tall, strong and handsome. And very inclined to dance.

Over the century starting in about 1750, Ireland was a perfect laboratory for the theories of the political economist Thomas Robert Malthus. His 'Iron Law of Population', first aired in 1798, held that population numbers increased in geometric proportion to available resources and that, if left unchecked, this increase would inevitably outrun those resources, resulting in famine.

Between 1750 and 1845, the number of people living on the island of Ireland exploded, rising from around 2 million in the mid-eighteenth century to over 8 million in the census of 1841. The potato was entirely responsible. As well as being nutritious, it was also very simple to grow and very forgiving of the poor soil and wet climate in the most over-populated Atlantic coast areas. A single acre could produce up to twelve tons of potatoes, enough to feed a family of six for a year. Two months' hard work, at planting and harvesting, were all it took, leaving plenty of time for dancing. And music. And marrying early and having lots of children.

In the eyes of their landlords and the English administrators, the Irish peasantry were lazy. The planting system involved so-called 'lazy beds'. All that remains of them are their humped lines, still visible on the sides of mountains or on waste ground by the edges of abandoned villages, like the skeletal ribs of a decomposing giant. The lives of the people who depended on them were anything but easy and certainly not lazy.

With Malthus in mind, the politicians and functionaries in charge of Ireland in the first decades of the 1800s, almost all of them English after the Act of Union in 1800, were uncomfortably aware of the potential disaster on their hands. They knew that Ireland was a catastrophe waiting to happen. And in the 1820s and 1830s, local famines and epidemics occurred regularly, in retrospect harbingers of that catastrophe.

In late July 1845, reports began to arrive of what seemed like another such local problem. Potato plants began to rot where they stood in the fields and a sickening sweetness filled the air. When attempts were made to save the tubers in the ground, they too were putrid. This was the first appearance of the fungus *Phytophthora infestans*, the blight.

That year, only 40 per cent or so of the total crop was affected and, though many suffered, no one starved. Relief efforts concentrated on helping people to survive until another crop could be planted and harvested the following year. But by August 1846, the blight had returned, suddenly, inexplicably. In Sligo, one peasant remembered,

> the potatoes were clean and good, but that morning a mist rose up out of the sea and you
> could hear a voice talking near a mile off across the stillness of the earth. It was the same
> . . . for three days or more; and then you could see the tops of the stalks beginning to lie
> over as if the life was gone out of them. And that was the beginning of the great trouble
> and famine that destroyed Ireland.

In 1846, the crop was only 20 per cent of the pre-Famine level. The winter of 1846–47 is still known in Irish folk memory as 'Black '47'. The scale of the catastrophe is almost unimaginable. Workhouses, grim prison-like institutions carefully designed to humiliate and deter all but the most desperate, were overwhelmed by a tidal wave of panic-stricken and starving peasants: by mid-1847 more than 3 million people, 40 per cent of the population, had received some 'assistance' from the Poor Law system. It was paltry and grudging. The doctrinaire market-forces philosophy of Lord Russell's Whig administration meant that the government was more concerned about not interfering with free enterprise than about saving the lives of the famine-stricken. Truth be told, some elements in British officialdom were taking what today's politicians would call 'tough decisions'. Real-politik saw the Famine as a solution to Ireland's problems, not as the problem itself.

In Sligo, ships laden with corn were leaving port at the same time as the streets and cabins of the town were filling with corpses. Small wonder there was a mad panic to get out of Ireland at all costs. People flooded into Britain, taking terrible risks to get cheap passage to America from Liverpool. On 3 December 1848, in the depths of a terrible winter, the *Londonderry*, a steamer of the North-west of Ireland Steam-packet Company, set out on its regular route from Sligo to Liverpool, heading north around Donegal and then down through the North Channel. But as well as its usual cargo of cattle and sheep, it also carried no fewer than 190 passengers crammed into a steerage cabin, only six metres long and three metres wide. Desperation to get out of Ireland was driving them to endure conditions that must have been extraordinary, jammed together in the freezing darkness without even enough space to sit down.

And then the ship ran into a fierce northerly gale and huge waves began to swamp her, spilling through the hatch into the steerage cabin. So the crew sealed the hatch, in the teeth of angry resistance from those below. When the *Londonderry* reached the relative calm of Lough Foyle off the coast from Derry, they re-opened the hatch. A contemporary report from the *Belfast News Letter* describes what they found:

> When the crew went below, they were appalled by the discovery that the floor was covered with dead bodies to the depth of some feet. Men, women, and children were huddled together, blackened with suffocation, distorted by convulsion, bruised and bleeding from the desperate struggle for existence which preceded the moment when exhausted nature resigned the strife.

In all, 72 people died in this single incident. It was replicated over and over again during those years, onshore and at sea, in workhouses and mud cabins, in the streets of Irish cities and in the fields where the crops had rotted. Even 170 years later, a residue of bitterness and horror persists.

The famine memorial, Delphi Valley, Co. Mayo. This memorial was erected to commemorate the victims of the 1849 Doolough tragedy during the Great Famine.

Previous pages:
The southern view from Ben Bulben. The cairn on the summit of Knocknarea is clearly visible on the left of the photo.

Superstition

The magical cow known as the *Glas Ghoibhneann* belonged to the blacksmith of the *Tuatha De Dannan*, Goibhniu. Her supply of milk was inexhaustible, filling and overflowing every vessel used to milk her and Goibhniu boasted of her prowess, as anyone would. So a malicious woman bet him there was one vessel the cow couldn't fill. Then she put a sieve under the great beast's udders. Poor Glas strained and strained to fill it up and eventually died from the sheer effort. But her exertions produced such a vast quantity of milk that it seeped up into the sky and spread out over the stars. And that's how the Milky Way came into existence.

Irish people are not particularly credulous or gullible. On the contrary, a long history of being lied to by respectable priests and respectable politicians and respectable bankers has left most people deeply sceptical about received wisdom. But you will still find many hardened builders who avoid touching an old burial mound, or money-wise farmers who plough a wide circle to avoid damaging a hawthorn tree. The hawthorn was sacred to the fairies, and the echo of that pre-Christian religion still resonates: everyone knows someone (who knows someone) who uprooted a hawthorn and suffered unspeakable calamities. Better safe than sorry.

The hawthorn is one of the most common plants on the island so this can make life a bit difficult, but superstitions (or, to use a less loaded term, 'folklore beliefs') remain close to the surface of everyday life in Ireland and we're used to navigating around them. Don't throw severed hair on the fire. Spitting on money will make it more plentiful. If you kill a swallow, your cow's milk will turn bloody. Thousands of these *piseóga* exist, many of them backed up with stories of the otherworld, all of them serving to explain and exert control over the unknown, like thousands of tiny pagan sacraments.

When W. B. Yeats came to visit his Sligo relatives in the 1870s and 1880s, the peasant culture that produced and consumed these beliefs was still alive in the day-to-day world, and it fascinated him. His sense of an ancient religion, millennia old, lying just out of reach beyond the facade of the everyday, stayed with him throughout his life, mutating into a very strange spiritualism in his final decades. But his *Fairy and Folk Tales of the Irish Peasantry* (1888) began the journey, and he made superb use of some of the beliefs and stories he recorded.

In his first book of poems, published the year after *Fairy and Folk Tales*, the poem 'The Stolen Child' uses the traditional belief in fairy abduction, the notion that newborns could be stolen and replaced by a changeling. What is clearly a folk attempt to come to terms with the grief of childhood disability and mortality becomes in Yeats's hands an invitation from the fairies to the child to join them in a Pre-Raphaelite limbo:

> Come away, O human child!
> To the waters and the wild
> With a faery, hand in hand,
> For the world's more full of weeping than
> you can understand.

This culture of *piseóga* went with the nineteenth-century flood of emigrants to North America and Britain. In Britain, it faded as the Irish assimilated. In North America, however, parts of it metastasised. Books such as D. R. McAnally's *Irish Wonders* (Boston, 1888) took stories from the folk tradition, dressed them in the stagiest of stage Irishry and inflicted generations of pain on us all:

The Glenn. At the foot of Knocknarea, this limestone chasm stretches for over a kilometre. With walls as high as 15m this is one of the most enchanting and atmospheric spots in Ireland.

It's well beknownst that the Leprechawn has a purse that's got the charmed shillin'. Only wan shillin', but the wondher av the purse is this: No matther how often ye take out a shillin' from it, the purse is niver empty at all, but whin ye put yer finger in agin, ye always find wan there, fur the purse fills up when ye take wan from it, so ye may shtand all day countin' out the shillin's.

Most people in Ireland still expend far too much effort denying to themselves the existence of leprechauns:

> Up the airy mountain,
> Down the rushy glen,
> We daren't go a-hunting,
> For fear of little men . . .

Maeve and Knocknarea

Knocknarea is a monolithic limestone hill that sits at the end of the Cúil Irra peninsula in Sligo, jutting out between Ballysadare Bay and the estuary of the Garavogue river. It is an easy walk to the top and has some wonderful views north-east to Ben Bulben and west to the Ox and Nephins, south to the Bricklieves and the Curlews. But it is what is on top of Knocknarea that brings most people there.

The official name of the hill in Irish is Cnoc na Riabh (Hill of Stripes). 'Official' is never the only game in town, though. *Riagad* (executions) and *Riogha* (kings) have also been suggested. The kingly connection is the one that sticks in the popular mind, because the 12-metre-high cairn on top has been known for centuries as *Meascán Méabha*, Maeve's Cairn, the burial place of the most famous warrior-queen of the province of Connacht.

Maeve played a large role in one of the two great intertanglings of stories that make up Irish mythology, 'The Ulster Cycle'. She was the fourth of six daughters of one Eochaid Feidlech ('enduring horseman'), a king of Connacht who went on to become High King of Ireland by the usual method of slaughtering his predecessor and all the other provincial kings. The final great battle took place in south Sligo, in the drumlin territory to the west of the Bricklieves near the modern town of Ballymote.

One of those killed here was the King of Ulster and when his son Conchubhar (pronounced 'Conor') Mac Nessa succeeded to the throne, Eochaid owed him recompense. So he handed over four of his daughters in marriage, including Maeve. (One after the other, not simultaneously. There were standards, after all). Unsurprisingly, the marriages were a little fraught. A flavour of Maeve's character can be gleaned from her behaviour when her sister Eithne became pregnant by Conchubhar after she had divorced him. She murdered Eithne, and the child had to be born by posthumous caesarean section.

An indulgent Eochaid then deposed the reigning King of Connacht and installed Maeve in his place. She promptly took the deposed king as her lover. After he was killed in a duel with her former husband (a long story), she married the man who had been the deposed king's rival for the throne. When Maeve was discovered *in flagrante* with the head of this man's elite bodyguard, Ailill Mac Máta, another duel ensued. Ailill then became king. And so on. They clearly led a busy life, full of boasting, killing, adultery, treachery, sex, feasting and, one imagines, a deal of puking.

But Maeve's fame rests on other foundations. It was she who began the most famous of the many wars fought between Connacht and Ulster. In the course of a bedtime boasting session (a custom still common in modern Ireland), she discovered that her husband Ailill was one stud bull richer than her. The only better bull than his in Ireland was Donn Cúailinge, the brown bull of Cooley, the peninsula where modern-day Carlingford stands. Maeve was determined to have the bull and thus started the war recounted in the most famous epic of early Ireland, *Táin Bó Cúailnge* (the Cattle Raid of Cooley).

The story is long and complex, with many episodes that have become familiar parts of modern Irish cultural identity, most centering on Cú Chulainn, the 17-year-old hero of Ulster. He fights and defeats the champions of Connacht one by one in single combat. The Mórrígan, goddess of battle, appears to him in the form of a crow, a wolf and a cow, to try to seduce him, but fails. He kills his foster-brother and best friend Ferdia after three days and nights of gruelling battle. He turns into a vicious monster, loses his mind and attacks the Connacht camp, slaughtering hundreds.

In the end, Maeve acquired the bull, but lost the war. Her nephew Furbaide, the child born of her murdered sister Eithne, killed her with a masterful slingshot from the lake shore while she was bathing off the island of Inchcleraun in Lough Ree. His projectile was a lump of cheese, a piece of contempt calculated to make his revenge even sweeter.

Is Maeve actually buried on the summit of Knock-narea? The events narrated in the Ulster Cycle are generally said to have their basis in the first or second centuries BC, soon after the arrival of the Gaels to Ireland. As the *Táin* makes abundantly clear, this was an Iron Age warrior culture, dedicated to conflict and personal reputation, and zealous about memorialising itself in immense, elaborate oral storytellings that eventually became the cycles of mythology that have come down to us.

There is every chance, in other words, that the mythological Maeve was based on a real individual. The capital of her Connacht, named Cruachán in the stories, has certainly been identified as Rathcroghan, a vast complex of unexcavated burial mounds and ringforts in Co. Roscommon, about 50 km south-east of Knocknarea.

But there is one insurmountable problem. The cairn on the top of the hill dates from around 3,000 BC, at least two millennia before Maeve's iron age. If she is buried in it, her funeral involved digging into, and desecrating, something which had probably been mysterious and sacred for far longer back than even folk memory could reach. But if anyone had the brass neck to do this, it would have been Maeve. Somehow it's easy to believe it of her.

ABOVE:
The cairn on Knocknarea, also known as Maeve's cairn. 55m long by 10m wide this was constructed about 5000 years ago.

BELOW:
The top of Knocknarea.

OPPOSITE:
Nephin mountain in Co. Mayo is the second highest mountain in Connaught (806m), viewed here from near Inishcrone in Co. Sligo.

FOLLOWING PAGES:
Benwiskin Mountain (514m) seen from Ben Bulben with Donegal Bay in the background.

The north view from Knocknarea with Donegal cliffs in the distance.

OPPOSITE ABOVE:
South Sligo seen from Knocknarea.

OPPOSITE BELOW:
Ben Bulben (526m).

PREVIOUS PAGES:
Streedagh Strand looking towards Ben Bulben.

Nephin seen across Sligo Bay.

OPPOSITE ABOVE:
The Garavogue River flows under Hyde
Bridge in Sligo town.

OPPOSITE BELOW:
Cliff Baths in Inishcrone. Built around
1890 this was a seaweed bath house for
Edwardian holiday makers.

Mayo
Maigh Eo

MAYO

Mayo is a big county divided in two halves. To the north and west, the ancient Caledonian mountains continue their slanting journey from the Scottish Highlands down through Donegal and Sligo, and finally reach their limit here, slamming up against the ocean. Exposed to Donegal Bay to the north and the full expanse of the Atlantic to the west, this part of the county has a character all its own.

The western coastline is gnawed and eroded into fairytale chaos: Clew Bay with its 365 islands, one for every day of the year; Achill's magnificent sea-cliffs; the topsy-turvy maze of tiny inlets, islets and peninsulas that make up Erris. The north coast is different. It has taken the brunt of some of the wettest weather on the island and vast areas of blanket bog stretch across it like a great brown desert, bleak but magnificent. Metres beneath the bog, near Ballycastle, lie the extraordinary remains of some of the earliest inhabitants. Almost six thousand years ago, some of the first Irish farmers, cattle breeders, cleared the forest here and built an elaborate system of pens and field boundaries for their animals. Climate change (and perhaps their own forest clearance) then began to change the nature of the soil and blanket bog started to envelop their land, their homes, their buildings. The 'Céide Fields' is the name now given to the area where their entire way of life was uncovered, perfectly preserved metres deep by the peat, like a slow-motion Pompeii.

The south and east of the county are different again. Here the rain falls on a limestone-based terrain and drains into innumerable small streams, underground lakes called turloughs that rise and flood overground in the winter months. The water eventually accumulates into great chains of shallow lakes: Lough Conn, Lough Cullin, Lough Carra, Lough Mask.

How were two such different areas fused into a single county? An accident of history. When the Cambro-Normans seized Ireland in the twelfth century, the great De Burgh magnates were given possession of Connacht. They very quickly adopted native ways, including the Irish tradition of the bitter family row. The so-called 'De Burgh civil war' in the fourteenth century split their territory into northern and southern divisions. In the south, in what is now east Galway, was Clanricarde – the dominion of the clan or family of Ric(h)ard de Burgh. The north became Mac William Íocthar, under the control of the followers of the son ('Mac') of William (de Burgh).

When the Tudors re-invaded Ireland in the sixteenth century, they set up administrative areas mimicking those already in existence in England. And when they shired Mayo in 1585, they just used the pre-existing territory of Mac William Íocthar.

The county name they borrowed from Mayo Abbey, one of the most famous monastic settlements in Western Europe throughout the Middle Ages and hence one of the few places in the region the invaders would have heard of.

PREVIOUS PAGES:
Clare Island at sunset, seen looking south from Minaun (466m) on Achill Island. This easily-accessed view point has a glorious 360 degree panoramic vista of the Mayo coastline.

Achill Head from Croaghaun (688m). At the
very western tip of Achill Island, Croaghaun
has the highest sea cliffs in the British Isles
and the third highest in Europe.

The Armada

The Spanish Armada is one of those episodes of English history that have become emblems of Englishness. A wealthy, autocratic, Catholic monarch of Spain, Philip II, attempts to invade England. He is defeated by the ingenuity, pluck and courage of the fleet of the Protestant Virgin Queen, Elizabeth I, led of course by the gentleman-hero, Sir Francis Drake. In Elizabeth's own words, she had 'a famous victory over those enemies of my God, of my kingdom, and of my people'. In Ireland, it has been seen a little differently. Apart from the fact that we have always regretted the Spanish loss, it was the immediate aftermath of their defeat that had most impact.

When their offensive capacity was decisively broken at the start of August 1588, the Spanish were pursued northwards by the English fleet, up the east coast of England. The severely damaged Armada then had no choice but to plot the most hazardous possible course homewards, north-west around Scotland and Ireland. Inexperience in navigating the north Atlantic gulf stream seems to have confused their pilots: by September, they believed themselves to be more than 400 km further west than they actually were.

And then the weather showed them their mistake. A great Atlantic storm, the western edge of an autumn hurricane, a terrific gale 'the like whereof hath not been seen or heard for a long time' in the words of one Irish official, scattered the fleet and drove its ships on to the west coast of Ireland. From Dunluce in Antrim, to Kinnagoe Bay in Donegal, round to Streedagh in Sligo, and Blacksod Bay in Mayo, from Galway city down to Loop Head in Clare and on south to Dingle and the Blaskets and Valentia – ship after ship after ship foundered on rocks, or grounded or simply broke up under the fury of the storm.

Twenty-four of them were destroyed. Most of the 5,000 or so who died went down with their vessels, but an awful fate awaited those who managed to make it to shore. The English authorities, in a panic over the possibility of a Spanish invasion, decreed the summary execution of all Spaniards and sanctioned the use of torture in pursuit of any survivors. Anybody assisting them was to be charged as a traitor to the Crown.

Only eight individuals survived and made it back to Spain. One of them, Captain Francisco de Cuellar, wrote a remarkable account of his experiences, describing some of the most extreme reversals of fortune imaginable.

De Cuellar did not have a good Armada. As the fleet was retreating up the North Sea, his command, the small *San Pedro*, broke formation, and he was sentenced to death by hanging for the breach of discipline. Transferred to the galleon *San Juan de Sicillia*, he was still awaiting execution when that ship, along with two others, was taken by the wind and smashed on to the beach at Streedagh in Sligo. Under the impassive cliffs of Ben Bulben, 700 men drowned.

Three hundred or so made it to shore through the pounding surf. There they were greeted by crowds of locals intent on stripping them of all they possessed, including their clothes, beating them into submission if need be. De Cuellar, clinging to wreckage, came ashore away from the main beach and managed to conceal himself. He describes drifting in and out of consciousness for hours, glimpsing flashes of hallucinatory horror from his hiding place: 200 English horsemen riding the beach, slaughtering his naked and defenceless countrymen; hundreds of corpses littering the sand, with shrieking flocks of ravens feeding on them; packs of dogs fighting each other for access to the fresh meat.

OPPOSITE ABOVE:
Fishing boat in Blacksod Bay.

OPPOSITE below:
Blacksod Lighthouse. Built in 1864 at the southern tip of the Mullet Peninsula, and famous for giving the crucial weather forecasts that determined the timing of the D-Day invasion of Europe in World War 2.

When he was driven out of his shelter by hunger and cold, De Cuellar wandered though a terrifyingly alien countryside, cold and sodden, with improvised gibbets everywhere, and met a bewildering mix of hospitality and unprovoked aggression. He was robbed at sword-point of everything he wore, and stabbed. Then those who had stabbed him dressed his wounds and fed him oaten bread, milk and butter.

After wandering for days, avoiding villages and settlements, near starvation, with only whatever he could forage as food, he finally made it inland to the territory of Sir Brian O'Rourke in Leitrim. O'Rourke welcomed him as an honoured guest, risking deadly retribution from the English. And, by De Cuellar's account at least (the vanity of a Spaniard, perhaps), O'Rourke's wife became infatuated with him. This may be the reason he stayed only two months, moving north to become a guest of the MacClancys at Rosclogher in November 1588. By December, he had had enough and departed northwards to Antrim, crossing to Scotland at Christmas.

But his roller-coaster continued. Attempting to get back to the Spanish Netherlands, his ship was attacked and sunk off the coast of Flanders by the Dutch allies of Elizabeth. Once again he floated to shore clinging to flotsam and lost everything. By his own account, he entered the city of Dunkirk wearing nothing but his shirt.

Several years later, he wrote his account of 'the misadventures of the Armada castaway' as a letter to King Philip. Gratitude for the hospitality of the O'Rourkes and the MacClancys did not feature. The Irish emerge from the story as little more than savages.

The grave of John Broderick at St Dairbhile's Church cemetery, Mullet Peninsula.

OPPOSITE ABOVE:
The Menawyn Cliffs, Achill Island.

OPPOSITE BELOW:
The Menawyn Cliffs seen from Croaghaun.

FOLLOWING PAGES:
Keem Strand with Croaghaun towering above.

Croagh Patrick

Ireland has been a religious place for a very long time. In the forty centuries before the coming of St Patrick, there were least as many varieties of paganism as there have been since of Christianity. Only some of them left visible evidence of their existence, in the passage cemeteries and dolmens and sacred landscapes, but other traces can be found in the lives and religious practices of many Irish people even today.

Take the example of Bonfire Night: as midnight of 23 June approaches, great bonfires are lit throughout rural Ireland, with food and drink and games continuing into the wee hours. The custom is clearly a direct descendant of the old pagan fire festival celebrating mid-summer, though it has been tactfully rebranded as St John's Eve.

Or holy wells, credited with healing powers. They are extraordinarily common. One survey carried out in the 1940s claimed to have found more than 3,000 in the country. Each is now dedicated to a saint, and the offerings and holy pictures and prayers for a miracle are framed in explicitly Catholic terms. But these wells were originally revered in pre-Christian religion, sacred because they were the places where water entered our world, creating small breaches in the stuff of everyday reality and thus allowing access to the other world.

Or St Bridget, deeply venerated in Irish Catholicism, as important as Patrick himself in the story of how Ireland was converted. Unlike Patrick, however, there is no historical evidence that she ever existed. Her feast day, now 1 February, coincides suspiciously with the ancient festival of Imbolc, marking the beginning of spring and held halfway between the winter solstice and the spring equinox. And that festival was dedicated to a goddess called Brighid.

But the most spectacular example of continuity between pagan and Christian belief is the Croagh Patrick pilgrimage. The mountain, in Irish *Cruach Phádraig* (Patrick's cone), rears up almost 800 metres high from the shore of Clew Bay to a perfectly tapering peak. Every year, on the last Sunday of July, up to 40,000 pilgrims converge to climb it in honour of St Patrick, who is said to have spent forty days and nights on its summit wrestling with demons sent to him in the peculiarly non-threatening form of blackbirds. Apparently snakes also joined in, and as a result he banished them from Ireland (the blackbirds got off scot-free). The custom of climbing the mountain on 'Reek Sunday' to commemorate his victory is said to date back 1,500 years.

The climb is not for the fainthearted. A full ascent takes between two and three hours, first on a steep but well-metalled trail, then on a long, relatively level path along the ridge of the mountain. The final part is a desperate scramble up the 45-degree scree-covered slope of the cone, sliding back down one step for every two taken. Because the pilgrimage is penitential, some pilgrims climb in their bare feet, with predictably painful results. These days mountain rescue teams from all over Ireland deal with the inevitable emergencies. Before the 1980s, when health and safety first began to weigh on the Church's conscience, the ascent was made overnight, with tens of thousands setting out in the pitch black and often in pouring rain. Doing the pilgrimage three times, we were told, guaranteed entry into heaven.

But the date of Reek Sunday corresponds almost precisely with the pagan festival of Lughnasa, half-way between the summer solstice and the autumn equinox. And the mountain was sacred long before Patrick – archaeologists have now found the remains of a giant ringfort circling the summit, surrounded in turn by dozens of small enclosures. The complex is tentatively dated at around 3000 BC, and the most persuasive interpretation is that the central structure was the focus of pilgrimage, with the smaller structures providing shelter for the pilgrims.

The mountain endures, unchanging, and remains the sacred focus of rituals and beliefs. Only the beliefs themselves have shifted and varied around it, like weather.

OPPOSITE ABOVE:
The pilgrim's path up Croagh Patrick.

OPPOSITE BELOW:
The view from near the summit of Croagh Patrick with Clew Bay on the left.

PREVIOUS PAGES:
Clew Bay seen from Croagh Patrick.

The Earliest Peoples

It is impossible to stand at one of the hundreds of Neolithic monuments along the west coast of Ireland without feeling a kind of vertigo, an intense awe. On the top of the Bricklieve mountains lies the passage grave cemetery of Carrowkeel, with fourteen separate tombs following the line of the mountaintop, their mouths aligned directly at the huge cairn on the top of Knocknarea, some 30 km north-west. It is an astonishingly beautiful location, its loneliness underlain with the sense that this landscape was elaborately sacred for millennia, but sacred to a belief system that has vanished completely, except for the stones.

The same is true at Derreentaggart stone circle just outside Castletownbere, and at the Poulnabrone dolmen in the Burren and at any of the dozens of wedge tombs on the Mizen peninsula. Our awe is partly a reflection of our deep ignorance of the culture that produced such solid undeniable evidence of their beliefs.

And yet we do know a great deal about the earliest peoples of Ireland. They were latecomers. By the time the first waves of settlers arrived here about 9,000 years ago, civilisations had already risen and fallen in the Americas, the Middle East and China. We were very late in the game. The hunter-gatherers who first came to Ireland seem to have arrived from what is now Cumbria in north-west England. They spread throughout the island, following the coast and the inland waterways as they sought food, hunting forest game, fishing and gathering what they could. Shellfish seem to have been a fierce passion – vast middens of discarded shells still make up significant parts of many Irish beaches today.

Between four and five thousand years ago, the first farmers arrived. They brought with them a culture that had begun about six millennia earlier in the Fertile Crescent of the Middle East and slowly travelled north and west, developing elaborate systems of animal husbandry and crop farming. The huge increase in population made possible by farming, and their settling in fixed locations, created a revolution in social structures. Now, food surpluses made it possible to have governing elites, specialised craftsmen, the beginnings of trade, and religion.

These are the people who erected the great stone structures. We know that their society was complex and stratified: sophisticated organisation of labour was needed to build them, and those buried in the Neolithic graves could only have been a small minority, an elite. In addition, we know they were extraordinary astronomers – again and again, standing stones or burial chambers are revealed as framing a solstice sunrise or equinoctial full moon, massively solid reminders of seasonal changes in the positions of the sun, moon and stars. And we know, above all, that they were concerned about death.

By far their most impressive structures were built to house the dead. Awareness of inevitable death must have permeated their culture – agriculture may have caused a population explosion but it also brought mass death through famines, animal-derived diseases and wars. From the earliest age, children must have seen death up close and repeatedly on a scale utterly alien to the old hunter-gatherer societies and indeed to us. The social need to contain death, literally to build structures that could hold the dead and act as a link to an imagined afterlife, must have been terrific.

But this is all just imagining, perhaps just rationalising after the fact. All we really know is that these ancient stones are still here. Still, it is impossible not to feel some sense of the deep reverence it took to make them, even if their society has left us nothing else.

Doolough, Delphi Valley, Mayo.

OPPOSITE ABOVE:
Slievemore (672m) seen from Croaghaun,
Achill Island.

OPPOSITE ABOVE:
Achill Sound at sunset.

FOLLOWING PAGES:
Looking south from Mweelrea.

A rainbow at the Croaghaun cliffs, Achill Island.

Opposite :
Blackrock lighthouse, built 70m above sea level on a barren rock 17km west of Blacksod. One of Ireland's most remote lighthouses.

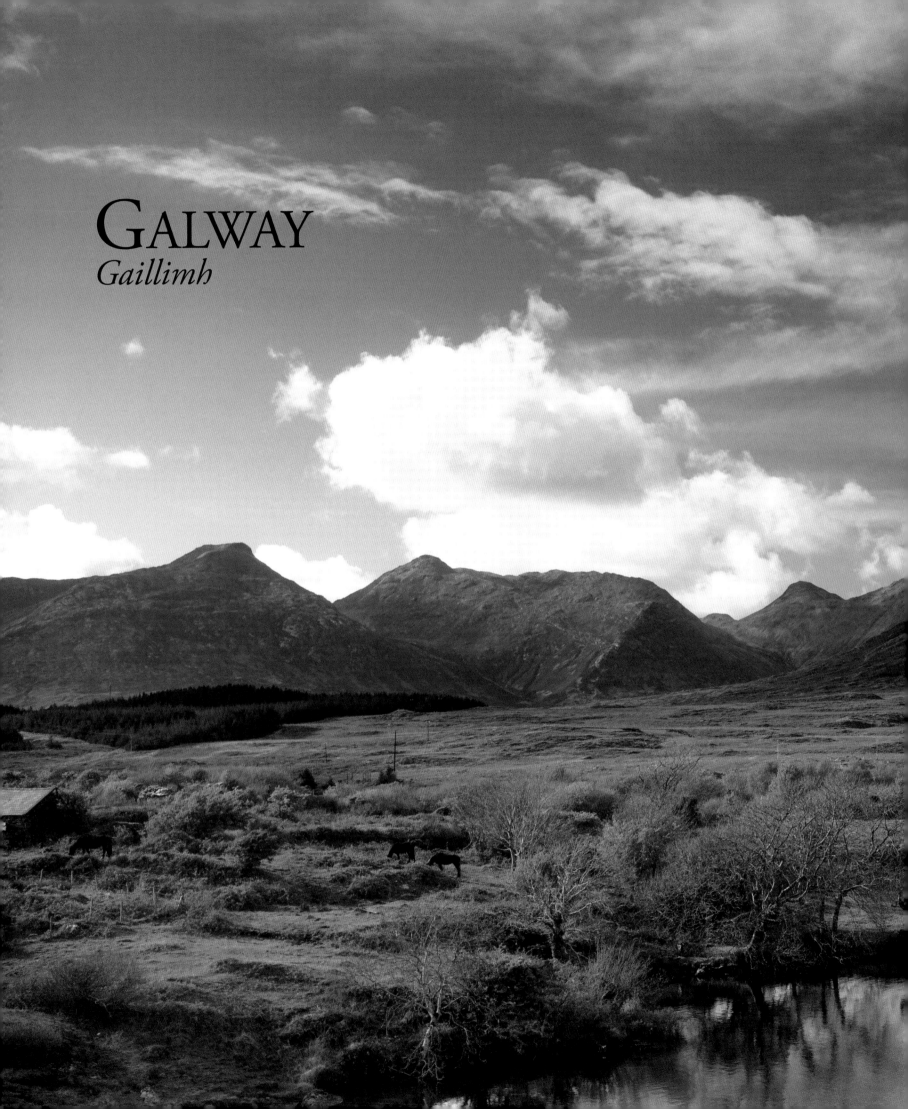

GALWAY
Gaillimh

GALWAY

Galway city marks the point where Co. Galway splits in two. To the west, bordered by the sea and the long shallows of Lough Corrib, lie the desolate rocky fields of Connemara and the terminus of the Caledonian mountain chain, finally reaching its end in the quartzite angularity of The Twelve Bens and the magnificent fjord at Killary. The east and south of the county is flat, riddled with small lakes and rivers.

The geography of the county has settled only relatively recently. In the winter storms of 2013-14, great sea surges ripped away layers of sand and stone from the shoreline at Spiddal to reveal dozens of oak, pine and birch stumps, all with accompanying extensive root systems. Archaeologists believe they are the remains of the woodlands, once populated by people, wolves and bears, that stretched out in lagoons and marshes to cover the area that is now Galway Bay. Around 6,000 years ago, a dramatic shift in climate caused rapid rises in sea-level, of up to five metres in places. The forest was engulfed, and preserved, in rapidly accumulating anaerobic peat and then covered by the sea. That climate shift is what produced the cool, wet, relatively infertile landscape of today.

In historic times, the west of the county was a separate territory, in the possession of the O'Flahertys. In theory, the Norman de Burgos, ancestors of the Burkes, seized control of the whole of Connacht in the thirteenth century, but the difficulty of the Connemara terrain allowed the O'Flahertys to retain their power more or less intact down to the final catastrophe of the seventeenth century. The encastellation of the rest of the county by the De Burgos was lethally effective. Despite becoming *Hiberniores Hibernis ipsis*, more Irish than the Irish, even taking up the bitter internecine feuding common among the old Gaels, they remained overlords of most of the county until the final collapse of the old order in the seventeenth century.

In the nineteenth century the British government officially designated most of Galway as a 'Congested District', suffering from overpopulation and thus entitled to special treatment from officialdom. It is congested no longer. A century and a half of hunger, emigration and drift to the cities has completely changed the character of the region.

Farming is not economic here – the small size of individual holdings, poor soil and wet climate make sure of that. But it is still the mainstay of rural life, taking the shape of upland sheep rearing in the mountainous areas and - a very risky business - outdoor cattle-finishing in the lowlands. In the scenic areas around the coast, seasonal businesses thrive on tourism, picking up where old seaside resorts like Salthill left off. Elsewhere the emptiness is palpable.

In a field at dawn overlooking Clifden.

PREVIOUS PAGES:

The Twelve Bens, or Twelve Pins. A mountain range of 12 peaks, the highest being Benbaun (729m). This range offers wonderful views of Connemara on the occasional clear day.

Tyrone House and the Anglo-Irish

Tyrone House, just outside Kilcolgan in east Galway, was built by the St George family in 1779, at the apogee of Anglo-Irish power in Ireland. The Anglo-Irish were a social elite who dominated politics, the law, land and the professions over the eighteenth and nineteenth centuries, generally tracing their descent from those who arrived from England in the wake of the religious wars of the 1600s. In ethnic terms, they could be of Norman, Old English, Scottish or even, in some rare cases, Old Gaelic stock: the key determinant was membership of the state church, the Church of Ireland. Many would also say that they also had in common a sharp eye for marrying into property, a love of flamboyance and, in many cases, a rough-and-ready approach to life, love and telling the truth.

Tyrone House exemplifies all of these qualities. It was a magnificent, square, stone-cut house, built on the Kilcolgan river, an inlet of Galway Bay, dominating the sea approach from Galway for miles, owning the most rugged views of the Atlantic, and housing life-size sculptures of the Lords St George, splendid stairways and marvellous plasterwork on ceilings and walls. It certainly succeeded in its twin aims: to impress the gentry and intimidate the tenantry.

Anyone who comes across the house now will not easily forget the sight. The huge Palladian granite pile sits gaunt, roofless and windowless, utterly out of scale in a tiny stone-walled field that is the last pitiful scrap of the huge estate that paid for it.

The evidence of the eye alone will tell you that these landlords were not well-loved. They were not the real St Georges, seventeenth-century arrivals from Cambridgeshire who did very well for themselves in the west of Ireland. They were in fact a family called French who married into the St Georges and adopted the surname to inherit. The estate that originally surrounded the house came from an earlier marriage with the Kirwans, one of the wealthiest merchant clans of Galway city.

The decay of the family came about slowly, over a number of generations. By the end of the nineteenth century, the widow of the great-grandson of the St George who built the house had retreated to a single room on the upper floor, where all the cooking was done over an open fire. Other members of the extended clan had claimed different parts of the building for themselves.

Edith Somerville, a wonderful chronicler of the decline of the Anglo-Irish, took the Tyrone House family as the models for the Prendevilles in her masterpiece *The Big House of Inver* (1925):

> Five successive generations of mainly half-bred and wholly profligate Prendevilles lived out their short lives in the Big House, living with country women, fighting, drinking, gambling.

Somerville's attitude to their Irish acquisitions is neatly summed up in the family motto she invents for them, '*Je prends*' (I take).

In literary terms, the book is most valuable for its extraordinary portrait of the central character, Shibby Pindy (Isabella Prendeville), the illegitimate daughter of the last great landlord, Captain Jas, and her obsessive attempts to re-unite the Big House with its lost demesne. Somerville uses her to dramatise the ongoing decay of the Anglo-Irish ascendancy, its slow absorption into the culture that surrounded it and which it despised.

Tyrone House, Galway.

But the first four chapters, giving the historical background to the main story, are a masterpiece of family and local history. Somerville was thoroughly Anglo-Irish, but also an outsider. In these chapters she is utterly in command of her raw material, the intricate genealogies of the landed gentry of eighteenth- and nineteenth-century Ireland, and she treats them with superb high irony and masterful storytelling. This is the complexity of Irish history as it occurred, told by a woman who knows her opinions are part of that complexity. And she never hid her opinions. When de Valera came to power in 1933, she wrote 'the powers of Darkness have triumphed'.

Her models for the Prendevilles lie in the extraordinarily elaborate St George mausoleum, just down the road from the house in Drumacoo cemetery. John Betjeman wrote of it:

> There in pinnacled protection,
> One extinguished family waits
> A Church of Ireland resurrection
> By the broken, rusty gates.
> Sheepswool, straw and droppings cover
> Graves of spinster, rake and lover,
> Whose fantastic mausoleum
> Sings its own seablown Te Deum,
> In and out the slipping slates.

Connemara

Connemara has always been an exception. Where it starts and ends is only the first of the peculiar questions it poses. Looked at on a map, the southern border, its coastline, has been shattered, re-shattered, and the fragments then shattered again, with the smithereens then picked up and strewn at random in the sea. On the land, it feels as if an unfamiliar dimension has been added to things. That hill over there, apparently an hour's walk away, will take a day's hard work to get to, through a bog desert, down into an unseen valley, around hidden lakes or inhuman moonscapes. Connemara's northern boundary is on, or beyond, or inside, or perhaps part of the most extraordinary geological jumble – great masses of sandstone, metamorphosed limestone, granite and quartzite overlap and push through each other, giant seams of lead or copper or zinc ore crushed and twisted by epoch after epoch into huge braids diving hundreds of metres below ground and then surfacing under bogs or in riverbeds or along the sides of mountains. Some mischievous God of Origami has folded down an entire continent into a few pocket-sized parishes here.

Before the great building projects of Victorian Ireland created the roads, piers and railways that give access to Connemara, this area was pure Badland. Impossible to reach except by sea, and even then only in very few places, impossible to cross, impossible to farm, whipped by wind and drenched by rain, it provided a few hundred square miles of perfect hiding. The peoples who came here tended to have good reasons for doing so. Almost all were trying to get away from something. The extraordinary structure of Dún Aengus on Inishmore speaks eloquently of a desperate back-to-the-wall defence and of the ferocity its builders expected to have to face.

Even the early medieval people who gave the territory its name, the *Conmaicne Mara*, were fleeing something when they first settled here. They were part of a much larger tribal group originally based in north-east Galway near the present town of Dunmore. According to medieval genealogists (mostly liars, it has to be said), they were descended from Conmaic (hence *Conmaicne*, breed of Conmaic), himself the son of the warrior-queen Maeve and Feargus Mac Roich, sometime King of Ulster and supposed original possessor of the *Lia Fáil*, the giant stone phallus used as the coronation stone at the Hill of Tara. When they were scattered from their homeland in the upheavals of the fifth century, unlike most of the tribe they moved south and west, until they arrived in these wastelands by the sea and could flee no further. They were then the *Conmaicne Mara, mara* meaning 'sea'.

You might think it's easy to defend what's worthless, but the simple fact of possession confers worth in the eyes of others. So the *Conmaicne* vanished, last mentioned in the annals at the battle of Clontarf in 1014, usurped (or absorbed) by the *Uí Fhleathartaibh*, the O'Flahertys.

The ferocity of the O'Flahertys was legendary, and their chiefs helped bolster the legend with blood-curdling nicknames: *Tadhg na Buille* (Taig of the Rages), *Murchadh na dTua* (Battleaxe Murrough) and so on. For almost 400 years they ruled Connemara, ignoring English law, trading wool for wine and other luxuries in France and Flanders. They forged alliances with the Burkes and Joyces, originally Welsh-Norman invaders, now gone utterly native. To the God-fearing, tax-paying merchants of Galway city, they were 'pirates and smugglers', but one man's piracy has always been another man's free enterprise.

OPPOSITE ABOVE:
The Twelve Bens seen from The Bog Road that runs across the Roundstone Bog Conservation Area.

OPPOSITE BELOW:
Lough Fee overlooked by the Maumturk Mountains.

It was only as they were losing power to the Tudor re-conquest of Ireland that they allied themselves more closely with the rivals on their northern border, the O'Malleys. The heir of the clan, Dónal an Chogaidh (Battle Donal), married Grace O'Malley (c. 1530–c. 1603), the eldest daughter of the O'Malley chieftain. This was the most famous woman in Irish history. Her family were one of the few seafaring clans along the coast, trading as far afield as Spain and Portugal, and as a child she is reputed to have cut her long hair to prevent it catching in the ships' ropes. Hence the name by which she is best known in Ireland today: Granuaile (pronounced roughly 'Grawnya-wale'), from the Irish *Gráinne Mhaol*, 'bald Gráinne'.

True or not, the anecdote certainly gives a flavour of her character. When her first husband Donal died, the Joyces tried to re-take a fortress in Lough Corrib he had seized from them and named, with characteristic O'Flaherty swagger, 'Cock's Castle'. Gráinne's successful defence, which included melting the lead on the roof to pour on to the attackers' heads, led to a change of label. It became known as *Caisleán na Circe*, Hen's Castle, and it still carries the name today. She married her next husband, 'Iron Richard' Bourke, under traditional Brehon law, which permitted divorce after a year and a day. Three hundred and sixty-six days later, she and her followers locked themselves into Carraigahowley Castle, one of Bourke's most prized possessions, and when he demanded entry divorced him by calling out the window: 'I dismiss you, Richard Bourke.' In 1593, she sailed to London and managed to meet Queen Elizabeth I in person to petition for the release of her sons and her half-brother, imprisoned by the English Governor of Connacht – apparently they spoke in Latin, as Gráinne had no English and Elizabeth no Irish. Although she got what she wanted, English encroachment on O'Malley territory continued and she rebelled, to no avail. By 1603, she was dead.

The ensuing English seizure of Connemara did not mean the imposition of normality. Even the largest of Anglo-Irish landlords in the area tended to become a little eccentric, to put it mildly. Richard Martin (1754–1834), a scion of one of the law-abiding merchant tribes of Galway, owned more than 100,000 acres centred on Ballynahinch. His wealth didn't do much for his temper. Over the course of a long life, he fought more than a hundred duels, earning himself the nickname 'Hair-trigger Dick'. He much preferred animals: as a Westminster MP he was responsible for 'Martin's Act' of 1822, 'An Act to prevent the cruel and improper Treatment of Cattle.' It was the first piece of animal welfare legislation. His passion for animals and ferocity towards fellow humans led George IV to give him his other nickname, the ironic 'Humanity Dick'.

Traditional Connemara cottage.

OPPOSITE:
The Twelve Bens, seen here across a lake near Recess.

Bogs

More than one-sixth of the total land area of the island of Ireland is covered by bogs, a higher proportion than anywhere else in Europe apart from Finland. Out of that total, a big majority, 1.4 million hectares, is aptly named blanket bog. And by far the largest area of that blanket bog is found on the Atlantic coast, coating the mountains of Donegal, Sligo and Galway, stretching desolate and monotonous across the raised plains of Mayo and Clare, softening the jagged bleakness of Dingle, Iveragh, Beara and Mizen.

Like all bog, blanket bog is an accumulation of partly decayed vegetable matter, acidic and waterlogged. Unlike its inland cousin, the raised bog, blanket bog appears to be mainly the result of human activity, or perhaps a combination of human activity and climate change.

Hard as it is to imagine now, 5,000 years ago all but the very highest peaks along the Atlantic coast were covered with birch and pine. Their dense foliage may have intercepted and mitigated some of the Atlantic rainfall, causing it to evaporate rather than drain directly down through the soil, leeching away nutrients. Or perhaps the climate was milder and drier.

In any case, we know that the earliest farmers cleared away the tree cover on the lower slopes to make fields for their animals and crops – recent archaeology has found unambiguous evidence of the fires they used. In itself, the practice did not damage the forests on the upper slopes. But it changed the equilibrium between drainage and rainfall. Perhaps the consequences took millennia to emerge, or maybe just a few hundred years of cold, wet weather tipped the balance. Increased drainage from the uplands washed out nutrients and clay, leaving the soil progressively more acidic. A kind of feedback loop emerged: the heathers and sedges suited to the poorer, more acidic soil decayed very slowly, thus encouraging over-retention of water, which in turn killed off any remaining trees. The waterlogging itself delayed the normal processes of decay further, so that a layer of peat began to accumulate.

Over the course of centuries the level of the bogs grew slowly, a millimetre or less a year, but always growing. It rose to cover rocks, tree-stumps, even field walls, reaching depths of up to three metres. The vast plains of blanket bog stretching, for example, across north Mayo convey astonishing desolation to the eye. Flat, dark monotony stretches to the horizon in all directions, speaking of death.

In truth, the range of life adapted to bogs is narrow. Low-nutrient soil, lack of cover, constant wet and relatively low temperatures all mean that only a few species of plant and animal can live here. But they are spectacular: asphodel, heathers, bog cotton, butterwort, the soft dense sphagnum mosses, purple moor grasses, black bog rushes; curlew, snipe, skylark and kestrel; dragonflies, craneflies, moths and butterflies.

Bogs inevitably played a large role in the existence of the people whose lives they bordered. First, blanket bogs were the main source of fuel for cooking and heating in most western rural households until relatively recently. Over the summer, groups of men would gather at parts of the bog traditionally associated with their family and cut the wet peat (always 'turf' in Hiberno-English) into rectangular blocks ('sods'), which would then be piled into stacks nearby to dry. Even well-dried turf burns poorly, slowly, with an intensely aromatic smoke, but it was essential to life for most people.

A classic Irish bog. (Mayo).

Bogs also figured in their imaginative life. At night, and over the seven cold, wet months, they were dangerous, alien, redolent of inhuman spans of time. Children who didn't heed their parents might wander into one, fall down a bog-hole, never be seen again.

And this sense of the alien vastness of time gathered in bogs was only reinforced by knowledge of the extraordinary preservative qualities of the sealed, wet, oxygen-poor peat. Tree-trunks thousands of years old emerge perfectly intact – 'bog-oak'. Butter buried twelve centuries ago surfaces perfectly edible – 'bog-butter'. And people interred centuries before Christ reappear with their features, their jewellery, their haircuts still recognizable.

In fact, most archaeologists think that the artefacts and corpses now re-emerging from the bog represent votive sacrifices, perhaps propitiating weather gods, or praying for favours, perhaps punishing rulers by forfeiting them back to the gods. One thing is certain. The people then, as now, knew how the bog preserves, how much older it is than any human life, and how much longer it will last.

The Stags, a small group of rocks at the western side of Inishbofin. Inishbofin, an island 8km off the Connemara coast, can be reached by ferry from Cleggan.

OPPOSITE ABOVE:
Aillebrack Pier Harbour, Ballconneely, Connemara.

OPPOSITE BELOW:
Roundstone Harbour. Once again, The Twelve Bens dominate the scenery in this western part of Connemara.

FOLLOWING PAGES:
Dawn on the Sky Road outside of Clifden.

Traditional island cottage on Inishmore.

Opposite above:
Kilronan Harbour. Inishmore is the largest of the Aran Islands and can be reached either by air or ferry from Rossaveal on the mainland.

Opposite below:
Inishmore Cliffs. The geology of the island is an extension of The Burren in Co. Clare, with vast areas of limestone formed about 350 million years ago.

CLARE
an Clár

CLARE

Clare is almost completely surrounded by water. It is cut off to the south and east by the river Shannon, Lough Derg, and the Shannon Estuary, and to the west by the Atlantic. This isolation has had a deep influence on the county's character and history. It has kept an intense sense of tradition and an intense pride in local achievements and is famed for its hurlers and traditional musicians. For some reason, it specialises in women concertina players. There are more in Clare alone than the whole of the rest of Ireland.

In the old Gaelic order, the region was part of the north Munster kingdom of Thomond dominated by the ancient aristocrats, the O'Briens, later created Earls of Thomond. They retained a good deal of power down to the nineteenth century, having trounced the Norman family to whom the region was granted in 1275, the de Clares. For a long time it was thought that the county name was taken from this Norman family when the modern boundaries were fixed by Sir Henry Sidney in 1565, but a local placename, *an clár*, meaning 'board' or 'table', had already been used to describe a busy, very level crossing over the river Fergus outside Ennis, and this is now deemed a likelier origin.

In the Burren, to the north and west, the dominant family were long the O'Loughlins, who built the tower house now known as Gleninagh Castle in the 17th century. It is a peculiar anachronism, harking back to the Norman motte and bailey constructions of five centuries before. A testament to the extreme insecurity of the 1600s, no doubt.

The county is now dominated economically by the conurbation stretching from Limerick to Shannon to Ennis in the south, which has attracted large numbers of immigrants, mainly from eastern Europe. To the west and north, small farms abound, uneconomic but for their owners impossible to let go.

The coastline is at the mercy of the Atlantic, with sandy beaches traditionally at the heart of old seaside resorts such as Lahinch, Miltown Malbay and Kilkee alternating with the dramatically eroded sea-cliffs at Black Head, Moher and Loop Head. The sea is winning. Every year a bit more of the coast erodes – the very end of the Loop Head peninsula will soon be an island.

Eastern European immigrants precariously fish for mackerel from the cliffs on Loop Head.

PREVIOUS PAGES:
The Clare coastline, south of Lahinch to Loop Head, has probably the most dramatic geological exhibition you'll ever see.

Emigration from Clare

The island of Ireland now has a population about the same size as Rio de Janeiro. The number of people with Irish ancestors outside Ireland is the equivalent of all the people in New York, London, Beijing, Mexico City, Hong Kong, Tokyo, Bangkok, Lagos, Cairo and Los Angeles combined. There are six and a half million of us here. There are more than 80 million of them out there.

The relationship between Ireland and its diaspora, the descendants of those who emigrated, is utterly exceptional. Yes, there are 50 million German-Americans and 'only' 40 million Irish-Americans. But 90 million people live in today's Germany. Germans outnumber German-Americans almost two to one. Irish-Americans outnumber us almost six to one. Compare us with any other country on the planet that has experienced mass migration - Israel, China, Italy, Spain – and that situation of disproportion is unique.

The reasons are nor far to seek. Like a vast exploding seed-pod, the great burst of Famine emigration scattered links all over the globe that, when they rooted, continued to draw rivers of cousins and in-laws and neighbours out of Ireland for almost a century and a half.

Pre-Famine Clare was ripe for that explosion of mass departure. The countryside was densely populated, the land was poor, and most of the farms were subsistence-level smallholdings. The Famine devastated the county. In the last census before the Blight struck, in 1841, 286,394 lived in the county. Within forty years, that number had fallen by more than half, and went on falling for another century. By 1950, the county had only 28% of the 1841 population.

Some of the initial drop was mortality – starvation and famine fever killed thousands here. But most of the collapse was emigration. Australia became a particular destination for one type of 'assisted' migrant: in the three years to 1848, no fewer than 4167 female orphans of marriageable age were sent to Australia by Ennistymon workhouse alone. Those who prospered provided destinations for siblings and cousins and whole extended families, and the links between Australia and Clare are still strong today.

After the initial desperate rush to escape the spectre of Famine, personal links such as these turned emigration into chain migration. A brother sent back the fare. A neighbour wrote a glowing account of working in Boston. A cousin invited you to come and join the California Gold Rush.

The feelings of those of whose ancestors stayed in Ireland towards our diaspora have never been unmixed. There is survivor guilt, still echoing down the generations. Our ancestors could stay because theirs were forced to go. There is also common-or-garden guilt. Those few extra acres they left behind came in very handy and we don't want them coming looking for them back, now do we?

And of course if they all came back at once, there'd be nowhere to sit down.

OPPOSITE ABOVE:
The Atlantic Ocean seen from Co. Clare. Newfoundland lies over 3000km to the west from here.

OPPOSITE BELOW:
A deserted cottage in Co. Mayo.

PAGES FOLLOWING:
Boulders resting on limestone paving on The Burren.

The Burren

The ancient desolation evoked by the barren moonscape of the Burren is not entirely deceptive. The great bare sheets of rock stretching to the horizon are made of carboniferous limestone, laid down as sediment in the tropical oceans that washed over Ireland hundreds of millions of years ago.

In those shallow seas, which covered almost all of the Earth's surface because the climate was so much warmer, single-celled sea-creatures just thousandths of a millimetre in diameter built tiny shells out of calcium carbonate. When they died, their shells drifted to the sea-floor. Think of the hundreds of millennia needed to build up even a small deposit of this material. Think of the eons required to produce enough weight to turn these deposits first into chalk, then into solid limestone.

But geographers point out that around 100 million years ago a layer of chalk more than 100 metres deep covered the whole island. Imagine that slow, invisible snowfall of tiny skeletons and then the sheer length of time required for it to produce and then compress a 100-metre-deep deposit.

And that layer of chalk has itself now vanished almost completely - outside the extreme north-east the only evidence it ever existed is a deep pit of chalk at Ballydeenlea near Farranfore in Kerry, apparently preserved when the limestone on which it was sitting collapsed. Otherwise every trace of the layer has gone. How much weathering, over how long, was needed to scour away such massive quantities of chalk?

For any geologist this all happened yesterday. There are changes in the rocks around us that record events 500 million years ago, a billion years ago and more. The oldest surviving civilization on the planet is in China, where the culture can trace itself over at least 3,000 years. There are Chinese families with traditions that follow their ancestors over more than 60 generations. This is extraordinary to our shallow Western sense of the past, but it is hardly long enough for even the lightest fall of chalk.

What we see in these limestone sheets are the most densely compressed skeletons, still enduring after the chalk has melted away.

OPPOSITE ABOVE:
Abbey Hill on The Burren.

OPPOSITE BELOW:
The Burren.

Of course, the Burren is also a living landscape. Deep crevices in the limestone layers, 'grikes', provide shelter for plants and small animals, and the limestone itself acts as a natural heat store, slowly radiating the summer's energy through the winter months. As a result, a completely unique network of miniature ecosystems has evolved, combining flora from utterly different climates, with plants usually found around the Mediterranean, in the Alps and in the Arctic all appearing side by side.

Orchids, alpine Gentians, wood anemones, juniper bushes, all rare elsewhere in Ireland, are common here. Their spring flowering is a spectacular display of beautiful botanical improbabilities, as lime-loving and acid-loving plants happily rub shoulders with woodland flowers out in the open, without a tree in sight.

It is also living in the sense that this is a farmed landscape. Controversy still surrounds the question of whether early farmers helped to expose the bare limestone sheets by clearing woodland to create pasture. But today's farmers are actively working to preserve the unique ecology of the area, as well as exploiting it: this is one of the very few places on earth where 'reverse transhumance' occurs. Instead of taking cattle to graze the uplands in summer, here the cattle go up onto the high limestone sheets in the winter months. The stone's ability to retain heat means that grass continues to grow in the Burren's fissures and gaps long after it has stopped in the lowland soils. And the cattle contribute too, not only with rich cowpats, but by cropping the scrub that threatens to spread onto the limestone. What goes around, comes around.

Limestone walls on limestone paving.

OPPOSITE:
Limestone paving covered with many glacial boulders or 'erratics' left during the retreat of the last ice age approximately 20,000 years ago.

Turloughmore Mountain, The Burren.

Opposite:
A limestone boulder balances on Abbey
Hill on The Burren.

Waves

Watching Atlantic waves shatter themselves against the coastline, with gargantuan spouts of surf and foam erupting in slow motion over rocks and cliffs, it is hard to believe that the water hasn't been building up to this final crescendo of arrival as it travelled thousands of ocean miles. But that's not how waves work.

Imagine a giant bull-whip stretching from Nova Scotia to Clare. When it is cracked, tremendous energy arrives and shatters into the coastline. But the whip itself doesn't travel. The wave moving up and down along the length of the lash transmits huge force without changing the whip itself.

So it is with ocean waves. A black February depression off Labrador flings hurricane-strength wind across a vast expanse of water, creating a resonance on the surface that picks up the storm's energy and transmits it westward. But the waves that carry it are motions up and down, not a straight pushing of the sea to the west. And even this up-and-down motion is limited: below half the distance from wave-crest to wave-crest, half the wavelength, the sea is completely unaffected by the storm.

It is only when the waves begin to meet the seabed near the coast that they change. The bottom of the wave is dragged at by the bottom, changing the shape of the wave, causing its top to begin to topple forward like a man carrying an immense weight who begins to stagger forward. The incline of the shallows determines the nature of the wave break. The steeper the incline, the less time the wave has to develop great height – a surging breaker travelling far inland and swamping all in its path is the result.

In the slowly shallowing waters of the continental shelf off Clare, the most common end for a wave is the spilling breaker, slow fringes of white water marching relentlessly at the shoreline. Slightly less shallow approaches can produce the surfer's dream, the plunging breaker. A spot a few hundred metres off the coast, between Doolin and the cliffs of Moher, has an underwater slope of just the right gradient. When the wind is from the north-west, great barrelling plungers rear up here, attracting surfers in suicidal competition.

But waves are responsible for more than just the great winter whiplashes that scour the coast. The Gulf Stream is the great, warm underwater current that flows from the Gulf of Mexico to the Arctic and results in winter temperatures in Ireland on average 20 degrees centigrade warmer than in Newfoundland, at the same latitude on the other side of the Atlantic. The pump powering it is simply the difference between surface water temperatures: hot water rises, cold water sinks. On an oceanic scale, this sets up a giant circular pump. What keeps the Stream as a coherent flow are the giant underwater waves, some up to 100 metres long, that the planet-sized pump produces.

As Joyce said when criticised for his unhygienic ways, 'All Ireland is washed by the Gulf Stream'.

OPPOSITE ABOVE:
Lahinch.

FOLLOWING PAGES:
Sunset from Hag's Head, just south of The Cliffs of Moher.

O'Brien's Tower overlooks the 70m sea stack
An Bhreannán Mór at the Cliffs of Moher.

OPPOSITE ABOVE :
O'Brien's Tower situated near the highest
point of The Cliffs of Moher (214m).

OPPOSITE BELOW:
The remains of a stone quarry on The Cliffs
of Moher with Hag's Head in the distance.
Quarrying stone from this area was a major
source of employment up until WW1,
when ships were no longer able to transport
the rock to England.

ABOVE AND BELOW:
Sea stacks and other massive rock structures
off the Clare coast.

OPPOSITE:
Notice the ruins of a dwelling on the summit
of this huge rock, separated from the
mainland by thousands of years of coastal
erosion.

FOLLOWING PAGES:
This enormous rectangular carbonaceous
lump of rock is at the very tip of Loop Head,
separated from the mainland by millennia
of tidal pummeling by the ocean.

A Martello Tower built during the Napoleonic War at Finavarra Point.

OPPOSITE ABOVE:
Gleninagh Castle, built in the 16th century, stands guard over the northern shoreline of the Burren.

OPPOSITE BELOW:
The Pinnacle Well. This gothic structure was erected in the 1860s to enclose a natural spring. The well is adjacent to Gleninagh Castle, which has its own holy well.

PREVIOUS PAGES:
The interior of Saint Bridget's Well at Liscannor. The well attracts pilgrims hoping for healing of ailments physical and spiritual.

KERRY
Ciarraí ·

KERRY

Kerry is the most westerly county in Ireland, thrust out into the Atlantic from the south-west corner of the island, with Brooklyn traditionally 'the neighbouring parish'. But, contrary to what you might think, Kerry is not remote. No, it is the rest of the world that is remote from Kerry.

Kerrycentricity is taken for granted by the people who live here. They call it 'The Kingdom', officially tracing the source in the Irish version of the county name, Ciarraí, from *Ciar raige*, taken to mean 'Ciar's kingdom'. But *Ciar raige* actually means 'people of Ciar', with no hint of a 'kingdom'. There were many local chieftainships that took their name from a common ancestor – the *Dál gCais* (descendants of Cas) in Clare, the *Osraige* (people of Os) in Ossory, now Kilkenny, and of course the *Uí Néill* (children of Niall) in Ulster and north Leinster. And many of these chiefs called themselves kings – the early medieval Irish aristocracy had few issues with their self-esteem. But none of the areas they ruled have ever been known as kingdoms, except for Kerry.

And the term is not recent. In 1565, Elizabeth I created one of the McCarthy Mores Earl of Glencare in the Kingdom of Kerry. It may have been that Kerry's remoteness – sorry, the world's remoteness from Kerry – allowed its rulers the exceptional independence that merited its being recognised as so distinct. For almost 400 years, after all, it was in effect the personal property of the Fitzgeralds, Earls of Desmond, and sometimes known as the 'kingdom' of Desmond.

But the real reason for the county's attachment to the title is the difference from the rest of Ireland that it embodies. The rest of us left a kingdom in 1922. Kerry was a kingdom before we even joined that one.

They have some pretty strong reasons to feel different. The county is rich and beautiful, for a start. It has produced one of Ireland's few true multinational companies in the Kerry Group. It is also very diverse, a patchwork of cultures deeply embedded in local areas. From the urbanity of Tralee to the deep back-country of the Black Valley, from the cosmopolitan nonchalance of Dingle to the gloriously old-fashioned ice-cream and sunburn of Ballybunion, Kerry sometimes feels more like an empire than a kingdom.

And then there's Killarney. The town is unique, the oldest tourist destination in Ireland, first developed as the centre of an Irish version of the Lake District in the late eighteenth century. Though the landscape here is rougher and wilder than anything in Cumbria, the coming of the railway to the town sealed its success. It was prosperous before the Famine and has retained that prosperity ever since. Nowhere else in Ireland has money managed to settle, generation after generation, the way it has in Killarney. This is what Ireland could have been like with some economic good fortune. Like the rest of Kerry, it is different.

To people from the rest of Ireland, Kerry people can sometimes feel a little too happy about being from Kerry. So we reflect the feeling of difference right back at them. Just as the French tell Belgian jokes, the Italians tell *carabinieri* jokes and the English (used to) tell Irish jokes, the Irish tell Kerryman jokes. Did you hear about the Kerry IRA man who tried to blow up a car? He burnt his lips on the exhaust.

Scariff and Deenish Islands off Derrynane Bay on the Ring of Kerry.

PREVIOUS PAGES:
The Great Blasket Island.

How Irish are you?

For a large part of the twentieth century, in the Republic at least, there was a simple way of calculating the answer to that question. You could just add how Catholic you were to how much you hated England, perhaps subtracting something for living in Dublin or for poor step-dancing skills. And Irishness – the pure, unsullied source of the race – was located in the west, along the Atlantic. A caricature, perhaps, but with some truth, and there were certainly people in Ireland in the half-century between 1920 and 1970 for whom a low score was costly and painful. This was not just our own blinkered chauvinism, however. Like many post-colonial states, we also aped the empire we escaped. So it is worth remembering how that empire saw us.

John Beddoe (1826–1911), one of the founders of anthropology, believed passionately in the power of objective data. He carried out a meticulously detailed series of measurements of human physical features – eye, skin and hair pigmentation, head and face shape, skull size – across all of Britain and Ireland. The aim was to clarify racial origins and his findings led him to produce a statistical 'Index of Nigrescence', designed to quantify how close people were to being Negro. Unsurprisingly, scores rose steadily as he moved from east to west, with the highest point on the index achieved by inhabitants of the West of Ireland. Prominent Irish jaws, beetling brows, sallow skin and dark hair provided proof of the 'Africanoid' origins of the Celts, and thus their essential inferiority to the Anglo-Saxons and Teutons. QED.

Beddoe was no crank: he was the founder of the Ethnological Society and a president of the Royal Anthropological Institute, a bastion of respectability. This was the mainstream science of its day, replete with bar-charts, detailed accounts of methodology and calculated margins of error.

Contempt for racist claptrap like this should not blind us to real difference. Travel from Donegal to West Cork and you will indeed move between groups of people who clearly have different origins, cultures, accents – some more striking than others, some utterly distinct from their neighbours.

In the Sliabh Luachra area on the border between Cork and Kerry – the name means 'rushy mountain' – live a people whose music, dance, storytelling, patterns of speech and way of life are all unique. The district has long been the source of much of what is now thought of as Irish culture. Even the faces and physiques of the people here are different.

In the 1960s an Irish-American from Alabama, Dr Albert E. Casey, discovered that he had ancestors from the area, visited, and was so struck by the singular nature of the people that he devoted the rest of his life to trying to understand why they were so different and where they had come from. Over sixteen volumes of transcribed records and blood-group analysis and skull-shape measurements later, he eventually came to the conclusion that they were more closely related to natives of the northern Caucasus that to their neighbours. The most Irish area in Ireland isn't Irish at all!

The notion of race is not absurd in itself. What's utterly toxic in Ireland or anywhere else is the notion of some ethnic essence that can be measured: racial purity.

OPPOSITE:
Mr. Pat Hickey, Irish man.

FOLLOWING PAGES:
The Great Blasket from Sybil Point;
Clogher Head.

PAGES 138–9:
Waterville, where the Kerry mountains
sweep down to the sea.

Irish Monasticism and the Skelligs

The Christianity that came to Ireland in the fifth century had changed radically from the simple peculiarity of a religion insisting on a single god, ignoring ethnic boundaries, and a promise of immortality in the next life that was attractive above all to the powerless and the oppressed. Over 350 years, that religion found its way to the heart of the most powerful state the West had ever known, Rome, first as the plaything of bored patricians, then as scapegoat for military defeat, and finally, most extraordinarily, as the state religion. From the mid-fourth century, the religion and the state became symbiotes, and the organisation of the Church came to embody the bureaucratic hierarchies that allowed Rome to govern at such distance from its provinces. Dioceses were originally Roman state sub-divisions, and by the year 400 were functioning as geographic sub-divisions of both Church and State.

From the first beginnings of Imperial Christianity, some Christians were deeply ambivalent about the relationship. In Egypt, St Anthony (c. 251–356) deliberately chose decades of isolation in the most barren parts of the desert, and his heroic self-deprivation and single-handed duels with the temptations of the devil inspired a multitude of followers, including St Simeon Stylites (c. 390–459), who lived for decades on a pillar fifty feet high. This withdrawal from the world became more elaborate and wilful as eremitism evolved into communal monasticism, groups of monks banding together to live and suffer and worship in common.

Over the years Ireland was being Christianised, from c. 430 to 500, the western Roman Empire was collapsing, as former client and mercenary tribes breached the boundaries of province after province and destroyed imperial state power. Most became Christian and the administrative structures of Roman Christianity – Archdiocese, Diocese, Parish – remained intact in western and southern Europe.

Ireland had no such structures. When the first missionaries arrived (one St Patrick, or perhaps two or more, or perhaps one St Paladius – modern scholarship has muddied the waters wonderfully) they found an intensely tribal society where kinship, cattle and oral scholarship thrived. The imposition of parishes and dioceses was irrelevant where geography was always subservient to blood ties. But monasteries, with their communal property, their devotion to learning and law and their (often hereditary) ties to the local chief and his extended family, were perfect for Ireland.

There were no towns in pre-Viking Ireland and within a couple of centuries of the arrival of Christianity, Irish monasteries had occupied that niche in the ecology of society. Monasteries were often built at tribal centres or at meeting places between tribes. The sheer impact of the change is still visible in Irish placenames. Thousands of places still bear names with prefixes such as 'Monaster', 'Kill', 'Teampal' or 'Donagh', all meaning monastery or place of worship. We Irish fell heavily for Christianity, and then adapted it heavily to suit ourselves.

We also embraced both ends of the monastic tradition. Hermits there were aplenty – the common place-name prefix 'Dysert' or 'Desert' refers to a hermitage, taking its root from the desert origins of the movement with St Anthony. Something about the heroic self-mortification of the hermit echoed the Gaelic glorification of the individual warrior.

Of all the monastic remains that survive in Ireland from that era, one stands out like no other: Skellig Michael. Purely as visual objects, the two Skellig Rocks are astonishingly beautiful. Seen from shore they are classic, simple triangles, a child's first elemental notion of how a mountain should look. Twelve kilometres offshore, standing on the edge of the deep Atlantic, they shoot 200 metres straight up from the sea surface.

OPPOSITE ABOVE:
The Skelligs from The Skelligs Drive, a winding coastal road running south of Portmagee.

OPPOSITE BELOW LEFT AND RIGHT:
Beehive huts on Skellig Michael.

The human history of Sceilg Mhicheál (the Great Skellig) is just as breathtaking. The Irish monastic imperative to settle in isolation and deprivation drove the founding of small monasteries and hermitages on small islands all along the Irish Atlantic coast. On the Great Skellig, this impulse reached its zenith in the seventh century.

Near the north peak of the great rock, the monks constructed fragile terraces over giant fissures and ledges; on these terraces they built seven stone beehive-shaped huts, two oratories, two gardens and, eventually, St Michael's church. The history of the retaining walls, essential to support the terraces, demonstrates the sheer doggedness of the whole enterprise. The east retaining wall has collapsed at least three times since the monastery's foundation, with the oratory terrace and the garden terraces also showing signs of repeated failure and rebuilding. The monks wanted the monastery exactly where it was.

And where it is remains extraordinary. Even today, access to the island is utterly dependent on weather and sea conditions. What looks like a gentle swell at the harbour in Portmagee can make it unthinkable to try to land 12 km out in the ocean, even on the newly constructed jetty, even from a large tourist ferry. The monks used at least three separate landing points, on the east, south and north of the island, so that they could adapt to the prevailing winds. But there must have been months on end when no one could arrive or depart. And this desperate, self-inflicted isolation was a large part of the reason they were there in the first place.

There is no true soil on the island, only a thin layer supporting a sparse collection of salt-tolerant maritime plants. For food, the monks had to create their own garden as best they could on the frail terrace around the monastery. Perhaps they ate the occasional sea bird. But food was virtually nonexistent.

There is no fresh water on the island. Cisterns in the monastery collected rainwater and God knows there's usually enough of that off the Atlantic coast. But even here there would sometimes have been entire months without a drop. What did the monks do? Died or went to the mainland, as simple as that.

There is no fuel on the island. Never mind fire for heat, most of the year even fire for cooking was out of the question. So not even gruel.

One thing the island has in abundance is weather. Imagine yourself in one of those seven stone huts between November and February. Sixteen or seventeen hours of total darkness. Day after day, listening to the shrieking storms break around the walls, horizontal rain or sleet making even the most elementary visit to the latrine a prevision of hell. Day after day after day. But this is exactly why they were there. At the edge of the known universe, on the verge of starvation, isolated in the hallucinatory horror of a north Atlantic winter, almost freezing, with absolutely no escape, the monks had reached their destination. Their pain, their sickness, their solitude, all echoed and re-enacted the sacrifice of the God who had died for them. The sheer ferocity of their belief is awe-inspiring, and now utterly alien.

And, of course, for those who found the monastery too cushy, there was always the tiny hermitage on the south peak, even more exposed.

OPPOSITE ABOVE:
Small Skellig.

OPPOSITE BELOW:
Towards the mainland from Skellig Michael.

FOLLOWING PAGES:
Dunquin Pier.

Gaeltachtaí

Almost all of the official *Gaeltachtaí*, areas where the Irish language is spoken, are along the Atlantic coast, in three major blocks, each with its back to the sea: west Donegal, north-west Mayo/Connemara, and south Kerry. What defines these areas?

First, the language itself. It is truly extraordinary, veined with deep seams of idiom that incorporate attitudes of mind pre-dating Christianity and coloured by a deep familiarity with the natural world. A jellyfish is *smugairle an diabhail*, the devil's spit. There are no words for 'yes' or 'no'; in Irish, life is always more complicated than that. Even its word-order is unique, with the verb coming before subject and object; in effect, an Irish-speaker has to decide what the action is to be before deciding who does it or to whom, a back-to-front approach familiar in the Irish civil service.

If you haven't been through the full mill of the Irish education system, and you'd like to have some mischief with someone who has, ask them if they speak Irish. Nine out of ten will hesitate, look a little guilty and say 'Well . . . kind of.' They'll have studied the language for at least thirteen years, and ended up, if they're lucky, with the ability to pass messages in public in a crude pidgin, and use it mainly to avoid being eavesdropped on while abroad. If you ask about speaking French or German or Japanese, the answer will be straightforward 'Yes, a little,' 'No,' 'Yes, I'm fairly fluent.' Straightforwardness about the Irish language is not an option for the Irish-educated.

The main reason is a deep-rooted shame. The Irish language was the mother tongue of a clear majority of the population at the turn of the nineteenth century, with more than a million people speaking Irish only. But already attitudes to it were ambivalent. Daniel O'Connell (1775–1847), the greatest politician ever produced by Ireland, was a native speaker, but actively encouraged the abandonment of the language in favour of English. His advice, backed by an English-only education system, was readily heeded. By 1851, only 3 per cent of the territory had a majority who spoke Irish only – and all of the now-surviving *Gaeltachtaí* were in this 3 per cent. A further fifty years on, the 1901 census records less than 0.1 per cent of the population as monolingual Irish. In effect, the Irish people decided en masse to abandon the language. This is starkly visible in the detail of the 1901 census. Household after household records parents speaking Irish and English, and their children speaking only English. In their children's interests, the parents had decided not to speak their own language.

As Irish nationalism gathered strength between the 1870s and the First World War, a language revival movement began, and became intertwined with the struggle for Home Rule (self-government) and then independence. The leader of the 1916 Easter Rising, the seminal event in the creation of the present Republic, was Patrick Pearse, a devoted language revivalist who coined the maxim, '*Tír gan teanga, tír gan anam*' (a country without a language is a country without a soul). No wonder we feel a little sheepish.

By 1922, when 26 counties of the island left the UK, the Irish language was still alive, but only just. Then the full force of the fledgling state was thrown behind *Gaeilge*: it became the first national language, all public servants were required to be able to conduct business through it, the few areas where Irish was still the medium of everyday life became these privileged reservations, the *Gaeltachtaí*, and Irish became a compulsory subject for everyone from the first day of primary school to the last day of secondary. Instead of nurturing the few surviving embers of the language, the Free State and then the Republic chose the pious pretence that it was actually a blazing inferno. But the language was truly alive only in the mouths of a tiny minority. The vast numbers who were officially required to pretend that Irish was their native language responded by pretending to speak Irish. Official Irish became a pretend language, a thin veneer of (often made-up) vocabulary piously spread over English syntax, English idioms, even English phrasal verbs.

The southern view across Dingle Bay.

And for a large majority of the legions now forced to learn, as if it was their mother tongue, a language being taught by teachers pretending it was their mother tongue, the Irish language became little more than a gruelling exercise in advanced obedience training. Vast ranks of declensions and conjugations and orthographical rules and lists of idioms had to be swallowed and regurgitated on command. Little wonder that inflicting this on four generations of schoolchildren did not revive the language. On the contrary, the policies of the Irish state finished off the Irish language.

It remains the first official language, however, still compulsory at school, and the *Gaeltachtaí* still exist, shrinking inexorably and steadily hollowing out: in a 2006 survey only 15 per cent of the populations of official *Gaeltacht* areas – fewer than 10,000 people – actually used Irish as a genuine community language. In the mouths of these native speakers, though, it is still something wonderful, its extraordinary richness of idiom and high civility embodying echoes of the Irish culture of a thousand years ago.

Although there are no monolingual Irish speakers – which is surely the very definition of a dead language – the number of people claiming fluency continues to grow, and the genuine affection for the tongue felt by Irish English-speakers deepens even as the failure of the revival policy becomes clearer. With the extinction of minority languages gathering pace around the world, perhaps Ireland is showing how they might be preserved in a kind of afterlife. Irish survives here, and will continue to survive for the foreseeable future, but in a strange twilight, part lifestyle choice and part Masonic brotherhood.

The commonest cliché trotted out about Irish is that 'it's part of who we are'. In fact, the acutely uncomfortable mixture of ambivalence and blinkered enthusiasm the language evokes in Ireland is more a part of us than the language itself.

Macgillycuddy's Reeks, with Ireland's highest mountain Carrauntoohil (1038m).

OPPOSITE ABOVE:
Low tide near Inny Strand, Waterville.

OPPOSITE BELOW:
Ballydavid Head on the Dingle Peninsula.

Emigration from Kerry

In February 1851, Timothy O'Sullivan, his wife Mary and their three children, Patrick, Bridget and John, ranging in age from ten down to five, were admitted to the workhouse in Kenmare, in south Kerry. After five years of the horror of watching their neighbours starve or wither away from Famine fever, they had finally given up their own few acres and fled to the dreaded last resort, the militarised squalor of the poorhouse.

The following month, Henry Petty-Fitzmaurice, the biggest landlord in the area and the man taxed most heavily to pay for that poorhouse, decided that it made more economic sense for him to pay the bare minimum fare to assist the inmates to emigrate than to continue paying for their upkeep in Kenmare. So at the end of March, along with 200 other destitute individuals, the family were marched the 80 miles from Kenmare to the port of Queenstown, put on board a cattle ship bound for Liverpool and given the £5 that would pay for their passage from Liverpool to New York.

The cattle were worth more than the passengers, so they spent this first part of their journey on deck, drenched by the rain and the bitterly cold sea-spray, most of them seasick to the point of death. In Liverpool, they waited to secure passage and, while they waited, lived in the unimaginably overcrowded slum that much of the city had become after the great Famine exodus from Ireland. Families slept five or six to a room, surrounded by unspeakable filth and disease, always fearing they might lose or be cheated of the £5, the only escape they had.

Then, at the start of May, when they had paid their passage and were finally on the quayside and about to embark, in a moment of distraction five-year-old John wandered away. Despite frantic searches, they could not find him, and they were faced with the choice of staying, with the loss of their passage-money and the knowledge of what awaited them in Liverpool, or leaving without the child. They left.

After arriving in the US, Mary immediately began to write to Liverpool police stations, orphanages, charities, anyone who might conceivably have come into contact with John, and continued to write for the rest of her life. She never discovered what happened to him. Her other children then had to promise her to continue the search when she died, and then her children's children and then their children in turn. Over a century and a half, the agony of the woman's loss became embedded in the family's story of itself, generation after generation, each one taking up and pursuing the lost child again, each generation failing again.

Stories like this, thousands upon thousands of them, are what lie behind Irish-America.

Sunset from Dunquin.

ABOVE AND BELOW:
Views from Mount Brandon. The cross is a
route marker for the pilgrims' path to the
summit, where there are remains of an
oratory dedicated to St. Brendan.

OPPOSITE:
Rocks to the west of Dunquin.

FOLLOWING PAGES:
Pedlar's Lake, a corrie lake on the Conor
Pass on the Dingle Peninsula.

Gallarus Oratory, Dingle Peninsula.
Presumed to be an early Christian church.
Its date of construction is uncertain, but it
may be as old as 6th century.

Opposite above:
Leacanabuaile Stone Fort near Caherciveen,
built c. 800 - 900 AD.

Opposite below:
Staige Fort.

Previous pages:
Inch Strand.

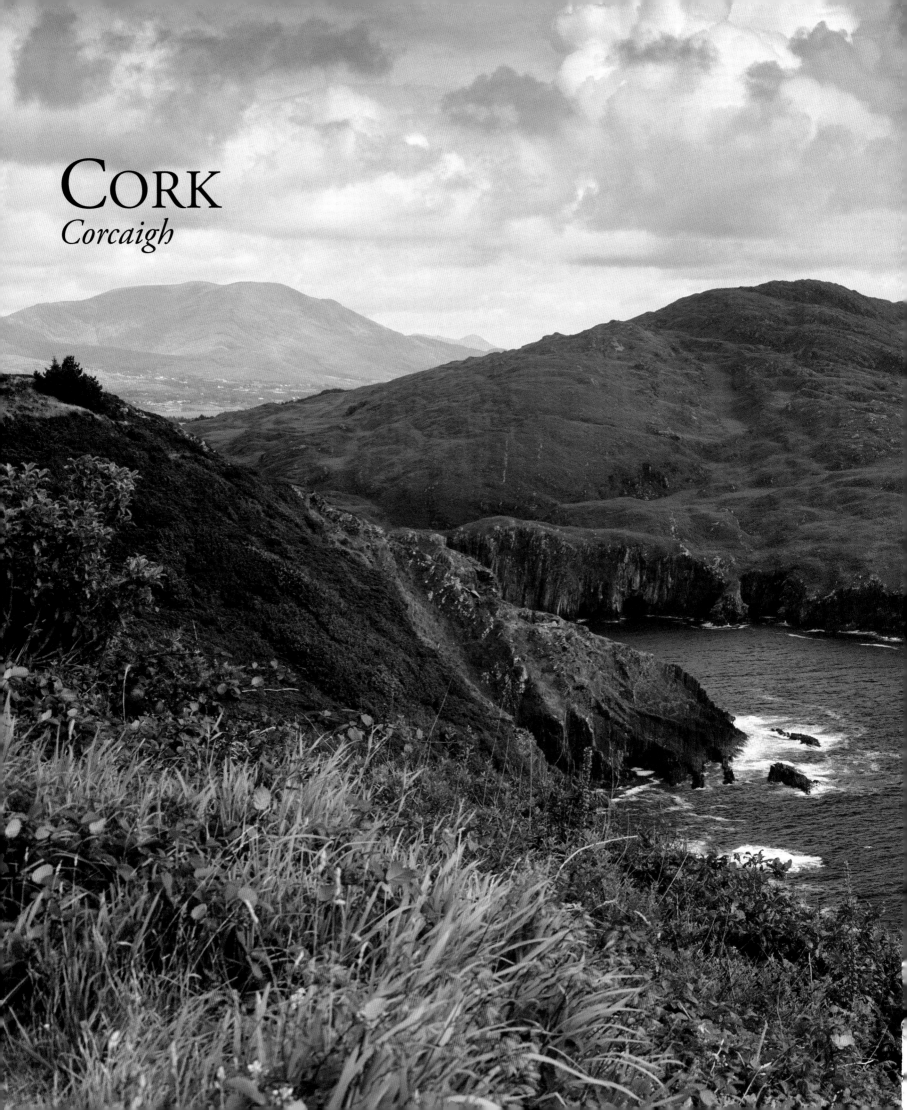

CORK
Corcaigh

CORK

Cork is the largest county in Ireland, and its size has had a noticeable effect on the mentality of its inhabitants; they sometimes refer to journeys to other parts of Ireland as 'visiting the Republic'. The county's Atlantic coast is very different from the lush farming territory to the north and east. In fact, although intense sibling rivalry will not allow their inhabitants to admit it, West Cork has more in common with South Kerry than with the rest of Cork.

As in South Kerry, barren magnificence dominates the landscape, with the spectacular mountains and long, jagged peninsulas determining and limiting social and economic development. The relative isolation imposed by this geography has nurtured intensely local loyalties and cultures, at the same time as making industrial development virtually impossible. People continue to cling on in places such as Dursey Island or Cape Clear out of pride and love of home, not to make a living.

Before the arrival of the Normans in twelfth century, the McCarthy Mór dynasty ruled the entire county. They had already been driven south out of their earlier territories in what is now Tipperary by the O'Briens, and were now pushed further west and south until their backs were to the Atlantic. There they stayed and ruled until the final collapse of the old Gaelic order after the Battle of Kinsale in 1601. The surname McCarthy remains extraordinarily plentiful here.

In the Irish Civil War (1922–23) showed the depth of nationalist feeling that persisted in the area and lived up to its nickname, 'the rebel county'. Most IRA units in Cork fought against the Anglo-Irish Treaty, and from July to August 1922 the city and county were part of the so-called Munster Republic. Michael Collins, the most famous figure in the War of Independence, was born near Clonakilty and assassinated during the civil war in Béal na Bláth, both in west Cork.

On Beara, Sheep's Head and Mizen, there are fewer tourists than on the Kerry peninsulas, but the two areas closest to the international airport in Cork city have many 'blow-ins', outsiders from elsewhere in Ireland or from abroad who have bought or built houses. Many originally came on holiday, but found they couldn't leave. The area's reputation as the source of wonderful artisan food – smoke-houses, hand-made cheeses, extraordinary confectionary and preserved meats – owes something to their presence, as well as the soft southern micro-climate.

Bantry House on the shore of Bantry Bay.

PREVIOUS PAGES:

A view of the Beara Peninsula taken from the Dzogchen Beara Buddhist Retreat Centre.

Weather

The Atlantic coast is the first landfall for the great North Atlantic weather systems. Driven relentlessly eastwards by the Jet Stream, these systems spiral slowly, warming up and absorbing more and more moisture from the thousands of kilometres of open ocean they cross. Until they hit the west coast of Ireland.

It rains a lot in the west of Ireland. This is not such a simple fact as it sounds. Yes, the most familiar (and dreaded) litany on Irish weather forecasts is 'rain spreading from the west'. Yes, there are entire weeks when it seems that a grey lid has been put on the world and misery drizzles on and on. But Ireland and its coast are not just on one weather border. We also live close to the Azores High, a warm and sunny feature of southern Atlantic summers that sometimes drifts up over us. We are on the edge of the European continental climate system and can occasionally feel the Siberian bite of winter easterlies or warm air floating north-west from France. We are uncomfortably close to the Arctic and sometimes, when the Atlantic conveyor belt fails, the North blasts us with ice.

So the main feature of the weather here is not rain (despite what it sometimes feels like), the main feature is variability. More than three to four days in the future, Irish weather is completely unpredictable. It can touch 30°C in summer and minus 15° in winter. It can also go up to 15° or 16° in winter and stay down at 15° or 16° in summer. It can rain at any time of the year for an hour, a day, a week, a month. Being an Irish weather forecaster is a thankless job, and the profession has developed its own jargon, full of defensive euphemisms: 'fresh and blustery', 'organised bands of showers' and, particularly common, 'unsettled'. Irish weather is 'unsettled' like the Black Death was an outbreak of acne.

One consequence is the peculiarity of Irish people's relationship to the weather. First, on principle, we refuse to recognise that it rains. Apart from the odd hill-walker, no one in Ireland owns raingear, and very few have waterproof clothing of any description. In a warm pub on a rainy day, the most distinctive smell is of wet clothes drying. And the Irish loathe wet summers; we take them as a personal insult, and are deeply, bitterly disappointed when it rains in August. Even though it always rains in August.

A more subtle adaptation to the climate may be the intensity of our desire to enjoy ourselves. When the sky over your head is a kaleidoscope, it is hard not to insist on having a good time at every opportunity. After all, who knows how long the opportunity will last?

That kaleidoscope is also responsible for one of the Atlantic coast's most beautiful aspects. The sheer quantity of moisture standing in the air gives qualities to light that are found nowhere else on the planet. Distances foreshorten or elongate, colours sharpen, mountains and lakes take on a tinge of the hyper-real. A passing cloud brings up textures on the surface of sea-water that are impossible to imagine. A slow sunset through distant rainclouds plasters the sky with lurid pinks, oranges and purples. Enjoy what you see, you'll never see it again. Something equally breathtaking, no doubt, but never that one revelation again.

OPPOSITE ABOVE:
Rain on the Caha Mountains seen from the Sheep's Head Peninsula.

OPPOSITE BELOW:
The north west ocean view from Mizen Head.

The Geology of the Peninsulas

The true north–south divide in Ireland is not between Protestant, Unionist north-east Ulster and the Catholic, Nationalist rest. It is something much older than even that ancient split. It is a line that runs from just north of Dublin, through Tipperary and Limerick, to meet the Atlantic on the north Kerry coast. Geologists call it the 'Iapetus suture'. In Greek myth, Iapetus was a Titan, father of Atlas and Prometheus, and thus a distant ancestor of humanity. His remoteness lies behind the choice of his name for an ocean that ceased to exist almost half a billion years ago. Its final extinction, with opposite shorelines finally closing on each other, took place along the line of the suture that bears its name.

North of that line the Caledonian mountains already stood, stretching from Connemara to Norway. South of it were vast plains, repeatedly flooded by run-off from the mountains. For nearly 100 million years, layer upon layer of alluvial mud was laid down, drying out, becoming heavier and heavier, until the sheer pressure of its own weight compressed it into rock, the sandstone that underlies most of Munster and south-east Leinster, south of the suture.

Climate changed, sea levels rose and covered the plains, and that sandstone began to acquire a mantle, first of limestone, then of chalk, deepening millimetre after millimetre, millennium after millennium, in the warm shallow water.

Yet another collision of continents then slowly began to work its effects. The slow crushing of vast areas of rock into each other deep underground began to deform the surface, slowly crushing great creases into the air, like a vast carpet crumpling. This is what made the peninsulas of the south-west: Dingle, Iveragh, Beara, Sheep's Head and Mizen, each with a central ridge forced upwards, flanked by deep valleys now under the sea.

Wind, rain, ice, Atlantic storms – all these worked on the exposed ridges, carving away first the chalk, then the limestone, to leave only the old sandstone exposed: Carrauntoohill and Mount Brandon and Benoskee and Slieve Miskish rear up in stark nakedness over the Atlantic fjords that now stand between them.

Unexpectedly, the least mountainous peninsula, Mizen, is one of the places that reveals the history of their sandstone most clearly. At the very tip of Mizen Head, where the sea has almost torn away the huge rock on which the lighthouse now stands, the stone is completely exposed. Vast purple-grey quantities of it now sit twisted and lifted at impossible angles, its original flat sediment surfaces warped and folded by powers and eons we can barely imagine.

Looking north over Bantry Bay from Sheep's Head Peninsula.

Beara

All of the mountains along the central ridges of the south-western Atlantic peninsulas are relatively young, at least compared to the mountains further north, between Donegal and Galway. The big difference is that the south did not go through the great glaciations, when kilometres-thick ice flattened and scoured the northern mountains, leaving them with cleaner lines, and protecting them from the atmosphere. The great southern peaks were created much later, but they've been weathering out in the open air for hundreds of thousands of years longer and they feel older.

Of all the peninsulas, Beara is the one that feels oldest. Perhaps this is because it is lower, more intimate. Up close, you can see where the wind and rain have eaten into the rock, where only nubs remain of what once were peaks. Much more than Dingle or Iveragh, the mountains fit into the air, or rather *these* mountains fit into *this* air. It creates an odd sensation, a kind of itch to touch them, as if they are more three-dimensional than they should be.

Beara also feels old because it has hosted so many intersecting and conflicting cultures. The rich veins of copper up at the end of the peninsula near Allihies were well known to Bronze Age metallurgists – there is evidence from 1600 BC of the fires used to crack the ore to extract copper. This could then be combined with tin from Cornwall just across the Celtic Sea to produce the bronze that revolutionised weapons technology. With the example of Cortez and the Aztecs in mind, it is not hard to imagine the devastating impact such easy superiority would have had. And the first place of conflict had to be here, where the raw materials for the weapons themselves were to be found.

Copper was also at the heart of another, more recent collision of cultures here. The Puxleys, an Anglo-Irish family who arrived in the seventeenth century, rediscovered the rich copper deposits at Allihies, and in 1812 set up a copper mining business around a peak known locally as Hungry Hill. It made them very rich indeed, until the copper began to peter out in the 1880s. By then, the connection with Cornish tin had been re-established and the Puxleys lived in Cornwall part of the year. In the early 1940s, Christopher Puxley befriended the author Daphne Du Maurier when she moved to Cornwall. He gave her free access to the family papers and the family history captivated her completely, leading her to base the bestseller *Hungry Hill* (1943) directly on the Puxleys. Five generations of 'Brodricks' are covered, from Copper John to Greyhound John to Young Johnny to Henry to John Henry.

The whole thing is lurid and melodramatic and a little snobbish, but it remains absolutely compulsive: Du Maurier was a born story-teller. A great tourism draw for Beara, then? No. The book is barely mentioned in local tourist literature, and with good reason. It is a little too close to the bone. The heart of the story is a feud between the Brodricks and a local Gaelic Irish family, called Donovan in the book. The problem is that Du Maurier followed the Puxley tale a bit too accurately. There was indeed a long-standing dispute between them and a local Irish family, the Donegans. The book traces this in minute detail, but depicts the locals as shifty, squinty-eyed peasants who can't be trusted. The locals still don't like it.

OPPOSITE ABOVE:
The Caha Mountains, Beara Peninsula.

OPPOSITE BELOW:
Hungry Hill, Beara Peninsula.

Beara also exemplifies the deep local differences between Cork and Kerry. A third of the peninsula, about 40 km south-west out of Kenmare, is pure Kerry: well-tarred roads, neat fields, self-satisfied water-sports centres. Like everywhere in Kerry, remote from nowhere. The Cork side is a different story: tiny narrow roads, poor signposts, overgrown hedgerows. Remote, in other words: you can't get any further from Cork city and still be in Co. Cork.

Yet another conflict here was between the old pagan religion and new-fangled Christianity. *An Chailleach Beara*, usually translated as 'the Hag of Beara', is the most famous ancient inhabitant of the peninsula. The *cailleach* is a female figure familiar in all European folklore, past childbearing but sexually active, feeding off male sexuality. The *Chailleach Beara* had a fine trick, perpetual youth. Seven times she aged and then became young again, and each time married a king, watched him age, rejuvenated and married the next. Things were going along happily until she riled the Church. She came up against St Caithighearn, the founder of the early monastic settlement in the Beara parish of Kilcatherine still named after her. Jealous of the saint's fine Christian cloak, the *cailleach* stole it and refused to give it back. The saint revenged herself for the theft by turning the *cailleach* to a pillar of stone, facing the Atlantic, doomed forever to have her former dominion out of sight behind her back.

Not a word of it is true, of course.

An old Dursey Island cable car upgraded to a chicken house in a back garden in Ballaghboy, the mainland terminus for Ireland's only cable car service.

Opposite above:
Puxley Manor, Castletownbearhaven. An Ozymandian relic of the Celtic Tiger.

Opposite below:
The mine workings tower over the village of Allihies.

Mizen

If you start at Ballydehob and head south-west, out through the banks of fuchsia bushes and the elegant roadside stands of cow-parsley and the straggling commercial forestry, things seem straightforward. Yellow gorse will make a startling contrast to the occasional flashes of purply-grey exposed rock. You will catch glimpses of small farmhouses, small fields hedgerowed with fanatical detail, tiny sheep on the hills, flashes of sea in the distance. But as you get close to Schull, resist the temptation to turn left, down towards Roaring-Water Bay, or right, up towards Mount Gabriel, the low peak that forms the highest point on the spine of the peninsula. If you withstand the urge (and it can be very hard), you'll quickly find yourself caught in a maze of meandering little roads, doubling back on themselves, rising, zigzagging, looping, intersecting each other again and again until all sense of direction vanishes and you're hopelessly, joyously lost.

The labyrinth of little boreens on Mizen Head exists for a reason. The roads date back almost 200 years, when this was one of the most densely populated areas in Ireland. In 1841, almost 20,000 people lived on the peninsula – its relatively fertile land, mild climate and lack of steep mountains meant that almost every area was habitable, and every scrap of land that could grow potatoes was used. The hundreds of tiny roads are the fossilised remains of the access routes those people needed.

In 1851, the population was just over 11,000. By 2002, it stood at around 3,000. These charming roads, the beautiful emptiness of mountain and sea and cliff and bog, what we now see as unspoilt countryside – these are all part of the aftermath of a catastrophe. No wonder visitors sometimes feel this land is eerie, or somehow spiritual. There are ghosts everywhere.

Sea Arch at Mizen Head.

OPPOSITE:
Mizen Head lighthouse, built on Ireland's most south-westerly point. The last sight of Europe for many travelers on the westward passage to America.

FOLLOWING PAGES:
The view over Garnish Bay looking north towards Kerry.

Index